'Gareth and his wife, Lizzy, are the real de[...]
years of experience, in *Stones and Ripples*, [...]
the principles he has learned in church planting a[...]
new communities for God's glory. I highly recommend this book [...]
anyone feeling that nudge to step out and pioneer in a new church.'
—**DR AMY ORR-EWING**, PRESIDENT, OCCA
(THE OXFORD CENTRE FOR CHRISTIAN APOLOGETICS)

'Church planting is an adventure but also a very daunting prospect
for all involved! Steeped in Scripture and bursting with practical
reflection on lived experience, *Stones and Ripples* will encourage
and guide anyone who seeks to respond to God's call to bring
the gospel afresh to local communities. May it inspire many more
ripples and contribute to a mighty wave of vibrant, new churches.'
—**PAUL HARCOURT**, NATIONAL LEADER, NEW WINE ENGLAND

'When you're doing pioneering work it's important to have a guide.
Someone with ideas but also the understanding that only experience
brings. They know the hard, lonely work of turning dreams into reality.
They remember the battles they lost, but also the wisdom won and joy
of responding to God's call. This is why this book is so valuable. Gareth
offers a resource that will inspire and guide you for the days ahead.'
—**JO SAXTON**, SPEAKER; AUTHOR, *READY TO RISE*

'There is no shortage of books about the entrepreneurial spirit
required to not only see the obstacles and problems, but seize the
opportunities and possibilities arising from the epoch in which we are
called to serve God. All too few come from the coalface, however.
I am delighted that my friend Gareth has put on paper some of
what he and his wife, Lizzy, have learned in various settings so that
we can learn from their successes, empathise with their struggles
and replicate that pioneering spirit, which is surely the only hope
for Christ's ecclesia, whatever church looks like in the future.'
—**ANTHONY DELANEY**, IVY CHURCH NETWORK; FOUNDER,
LAUNCH CHURCH MULTIPLICATION CATALYST

'Honest, authentic, accessible. I love Gareth's travel guide of his ten principles for church planters and pioneers. Packed full of the insights of a practitioner, dreams of a pioneer and a worship-leader's love for Jesus. Simply put: "Turns out taking Jesus at his word actually works".'

—**RT REVD DR JILL DUFF**, BISHOP OF LANCASTER WITH OVERSIGHT OF CHURCH PLANTING, MISSION AND EVANGELISM IN THE DIOCESE OF BLACKBURN; NEW WINE TRUSTEE

'Are you ready to create ripples? This is such a timely read in a season of the Lord writing a radical new story in his body, the church. If you sense the Lord stirring you with a new vision, and you are wondering what next, this book is invaluable.'

—**ANNE CALVER**, ASSOCIATE MINISTER, STANMORE BAPTIST CHURCH; CO-AUTHOR, *UNLEASHED*

'*Stones and Ripple*s is an inspiring and brilliantly practical guide for church planters, written by one of the best pioneers and practitioners I know. If you're about to embark on a church-planting adventure, you won't regret grabbing a copy of this essential travel guide.'

—**PETE HUGHES**, SENIOR PASTOR, KING'S CROSS CHURCH (KXC), LONDON; AUTHOR, *ALL THINGS NEW*

'Gareth describes his book, *Stones and Ripples*, as a kind of travel guide. And a travel guide it is indeed – one that any serious traveller in the world of church multiplication will want to keep handy and refer to continually. There are other guides churned out by "theorists" who confidently share what other "experts" have said. Gareth writes from the perspective of one who has actually had the courage to go on the journey. That's the kind of guide I want.'

—**GARY BEST**, CHURCH PLANTER; FOUNDING NATIONAL TEAM LEADER, VINEYARD CHURCHES CANADA; AUTHOR, *NATURALLY SUPERNATURAL* AND *WHERE JOY IS FOUND*

'Gareth Robinson brilliantly gives simple principles and steps for church planters to follow, but then challenges us to dream big for a multiplying movement. *Stones and Ripples* would be highly beneficial to every church planter and their team.'
—**DAVE FERGUSON**, LEAD PASTOR, COMMUNITY CHRISTIAN CHURCH; AUTHOR, *HERO MAKER: FIVE ESSENTIAL PRACTICES FOR LEADERS TO MULTIPLY LEADERS*

'*Stones and Ripples* is a great resource for pioneers and planters. It is packed full of essential building blocks around starting and growing a missional community or church plant, and actionable and effective ideas. Gareth writes openly and honestly with an easy-to-read conversational style, bringing fun and humour alongside deep truth. He's able to shine a light on what should be obvious, but isn't always, and a number of times I found myself pausing and thinking, *oh, yes ... that's so true*. This resource is a must-have if you are thinking about or have already begun planting a missional community. Thought-provoking, practical and with much lived-out wisdom within its pages, this is a book I will be recommending to others.'
—**NESS WILSON**, TEAM LEADER, OPEN HEAVEN CHURCH

'There are many things about Gareth and his wife, Lizzy, that I love and respect. I have learnt so much from their honesty around the struggles and battles of planting. I have been inspired and moved to action by the way they modelled incarnational mission on a tough Stockport estate and how they consistently prioritise the most downtrodden to this day. It speaks volumes that two such impressive national leaders have also raised kids who really love them, really love Jesus, and fully know they are part of any calling to plant churches as well. So, it's no surprise that this book is full of gold, and its pages are filled with pace, humour, humility and integrity. A perfect read for activists, *Stones and Ripples* will challenge you to prioritise prayer and personal character over efficiency and action. This is the kind of travel companion you're going to want to keep in your back pocket as you head out on your own church-planting adventure.'

—**MIRIAM SWANSON**, GLOBAL STUDENT MISSION LEADER, FUSION MOVEMENT

'It's said, "those who can, do, but those who can't, teach". As an accomplished practitioner who has taught many others the principles of church planting, Gareth Robinson does both. At a time when interest in church planting has never been greater, *Stones and Ripples* is a much-needed resource of wisdom for the church, gathered by Gareth and his wife, Lizzy, over years of fruitful ministry. Whether you're a church-planting dreamer, doer, donor, director or don't know, this book is for you.'

—**REVD DR CHRISTIAN SELVARATNAM**, DIRECTOR, THE ST HILD CENTRE FOR CHURCH PLANTING

'Gareth and his wife, Lizzy, are brave, wise, faith-filled church planters and pioneers, who know what it is to turn vision into action. I am delighted that Gareth has set down some of the principles and thinking, along with the practical experience, that have shaped him and the church he leads. *Stones and Ripples* is an excellent read, and will be a helpful reference book for many church planters.'

—**ARCHIE COATES**, VICAR, ST PETER'S, BRIGHTON

'This book is gold dust, full of excellent ideas and principles, and all backed up with personal experience. If you or your church are thinking or dreaming of planting or enabling a plant to happen, I would highly recommend this book as a must-read. It's honest, real, inspiring and packed with wisdom.'

— **MARK MELLUISH**, LEADER OF A FAMILY OF CHURCHES AND PLANTS IN WEST LONDON

'Gareth Robinson has drawn on his considerable experience of planting missional churches and the wisdom gained from deep reflection on Scripture and practice to produce an exceptional resource for anyone contemplating or already engaged in church planting. Far more than simply a "how to" manual, though packed with practical ideas, this exploration of the core principles undergirding all missional initiatives focuses on those formational dispositions and practices which are vital to fruitfulness. A gem of a book!'

—**IAN PARKINSON**, LEADERSHIP SPECIALIST, CPAS

'*Stones and Ripples* is a practical, refreshing and humble perspective on church planting from someone who has had experience of building church from scratch. It oozes integrity and practical wisdom. Gareth importantly talks about growing the leader as well as the church and offers personal insights and experiences into his own journey as well as that of the community. Whether you are planting a large resource church or starting small in an urban priority area, you will find encouragement and wisdom here.'

—**DAVE MITCHELL**, LEAD PASTOR,
WOODLANDS CHURCH, BRISTOL

'In *Stones and Ripples*, Gareth Robinson has given us a guide book for the journey of planting a church. It's packed full of field-tested wisdom and stories that will inform and inspire you. Gareth walks the talk, and his ten principles equip leaders for their own personal journey as well as the practicalities of planting. Read this book and you might just find yourself planting a new church.'

—**JOHN MCGINLEY**, VICAR, HOLY TRINITY CHURCH, LEICESTER

'This is such a down-to-earth, practical approach to church planting and multiplication, with an important reminder that we must first and foremost be rooted in prayer and directed by the Holy Spirit. With different stories from both Gareth's own and others' experience, this book will enable the reader to think through their particular context and apply the principles and ideas appropriately.'

—**LINDA MASLEN**, CHURCH LEADER,
FOUNTAINS CHURCH, BRADFORD

'Gareth shares lessons from diverse journeys and contexts in this timely book on pioneering and planting. Using an inspired framework of "stones" and "ripples", he explores five characteristics and five steps that mine the gold of key missional principles with elegant, practical simplicity. Written in an easy, conversational style, spiced with stories and biblical wisdom and with challenging application questions throughout, this is a valuable guidebook for church planting and pioneering praxis.'

—**BOB HOPKINS**, CO-LEADER OF ANGLICAN CHURCH PLANTING INITIATIVES

'Church planting is exciting, challenging and complex. Church planters and their teams need help to harness that excitement, navigate the challenges and discern the complexities. Gareth's timely book is a welcome contribution giving essential principles for this growing movement. His style is conversational and readable, the theology is lived out in practice and it is highly applicable. Read, digest and use!'

—**RIC THORPE,** BISHOP OF ISLINGTON; DIRECTOR, GREGORY CENTRE FOR CHURCH MULTIPLICATION; CHAIR, FRESH EXPRESSIONS

Stones and Ripples

10 PRINCIPLES FOR PIONEERS
AND CHURCH PLANTERS

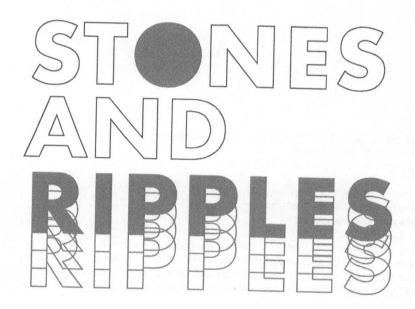

STONES AND RIPPLES

GARETH ROBINSON

Foreword by Archbishop Justin Welby
Afterword by Alan Hirsch

100
MOVEMENTS
PUBLISHING

First published in 2021 by 100 Movements Publishing
www.100Mpublishing.com
Copyright © 2021 by Gareth Robinson

www.100Mpublishing.com
www.movementleaderscollective.com
www.catalysechange.org

ISBN 978-1-7355988-1-9

Cover design by Kate Lehane
Cover jacket design and interior design by Revo Creative Ltd

100 Movements Publishing
An imprint of Movement Leaders Collective
Cody, Wyoming

To Lizzy, Daisy, Lucy and Toby: my family on mission.

Contents

Contents

Foreword

Archbishop Justin Welby

The other year I met someone who had been a *Great British Bake Off* finalist. I was visiting a diocese, and their organisers had put together an evening with this now-famous baker. Lots of people had got themselves a ticket and had come along. Unfortunately, I was the only person who hadn't watched the programme. The reason was not because I don't like cake. It's true I might not be much of a baker myself, but I do know a good coffee and walnut cake when I taste one. No, the reason I can't enjoy programmes like *Bake Off* is because I can't bear it when someone has to leave. It's too hard to watch as they exit the show despondent and heartbroken after giving it all they could.

Gareth has written us a book similar to an enticing recipe book. But it's like one of those great ones: not just full of words and instructions for making something as if it's a science experiment. It's one that paints pictures and gives context, which gives perspective and stirs your heart. And, most powerfully, it gives you a taste – in this case, for pioneering and planting in practice.

I'm glad he has written this book. In it you will find wise and honest reflections about the conditions that are vital for any church planter – characteristics that you can't just get down from the shelf, but which are part of the way the whole thing is made. Once he has set out the conditions – then we hear about the necessary ingredients, the steps, for anyone called to plant a church. It's clear, it's candid and it's compelling.

And because we need those who are gifted, called and willing to take up this mantle of planting churches, we need books like this. Gareth is like one of the expert bakers who isn't there to judge – but to get alongside, to coach and advise, train and encourage. This book could save an awful amount of time and energy for those at the beginning of the pioneering journey. Putting into practice the lessons Gareth has learned could only be of the greatest help.

I'm proud to serve Christ alongside Gareth and his wife, Lizzy.

Introduction

How We Got Here

I've always been a dreamer. Imagining how things could be – or even should be – and aching to be involved in something worthwhile. The idea of church planting has always had me hooked.

If you're a dreamer, dreaming about planting a church, this book is for you. If you're a doer, someone in the midst of church planting, it's for you too. You might be a donor, leading a church that wants to plant out. My hope is that this book will also help you get your church to that point of multiplication. Or you may be a director, someone working within a denomination or organisation wanting to encourage church planting in a structural, strategic way. I hope you'll find some inspiration for developing leadership pipelines and planting strategies.

But you might fit the other category: the don't knows. You're welcome too. I hope you will find some interesting thoughts, some inspiration, some honesty, and get to the end of the book thinking you might just give something new a go.

Let's start with the dreamers: me, aged sixteen.

There I was, attending church-planting seminars at Spring Harvest, furiously taking notes. Church planters like Roger Ellis, who had planted Revelation Church at the age of nineteen, were my heroes. By twenty-one, I was part of a planting team, excited to be on the adventure of creating church spaces for those who were coming to faith in Jesus for the very first time.

I learned so much from that experience – from what it means to research a local area, to praying into the spiritual atmosphere of a place and people group, to considering how to share the gospel with them … right through to what it's like setting up a room for worship.

Every. Single. Week.

(Whereas church planting sounded pretty straightforward in a sixty-minute seminar, it was a bit harder in practice.)

Eventually my love for music took me into worship leading, and I started serving at a church in Sheffield, St Thomas' Crookes. Through various connections I met Lizzy, and she moved from London so we could marry and start a life together. The group of young adults we belonged to grew and multiplied a number of times in a really healthy way. I got to see from the inside what growth and multiplication looked like.

And I also got to see that it can be costly. Every time a group multiplies, relationships change – something that can't be avoided, but must be navigated.

The church in Sheffield grew, and we moved into the city centre, eventually meeting in an old nightclub called The Roxy. Sticky carpets and everything.

And Lizzy grew too, expectant with our first child. We wanted to buy a house to raise our kids, but there was one problem – we couldn't afford to buy a house near the church, where the office was still based. We started researching residential areas near the city centre, and decided to move close to The Roxy, but we didn't want to do it alone. We talked and prayed with some friends and decided to move together to be a missional community in the area.[1] Three couples, seeing what God might do through us. And a year or so later, there were around thirty of us.

Turns out taking Jesus at his word actually works.

We started setting up spaces for worship again, a church plant within a church. Eventually we took on leadership of the young adult congregation, reaching out to the creatives and artists in the city. The church was structured to have small missional communities, which would be part of a larger congregation, and the various different congregations made up the whole church. So Lizzy and I were leading multiple little churches within one congregation of young adults, all of which were growing and multiplying.

Then we moved to America.

America and Back Again

We spent five years in the States, serving in two different mega-churches to help them develop a discipleship culture, alongside my role as worship pastor. And in both places, we started missional communities that grew as we saw people coming to faith in Jesus. A friend was planning to plant churches up and down the West Coast, and I was keen to get involved. He welcomed the idea of me being the worship pastor for the church plant, but, after all I'd told him about our experiences, he said he'd like us to plant and lead a church within three years.

Something happened within me. It was like the balance tipped from my primary focus being worship leading to community leading.

We spent some time in Orange County and San Diego County, and I distinctly remember one particularly beautiful summer's evening. The sun was beginning to set over the Pacific Ocean, and as we watched the surfers making the last of the evening light, I recall turning to Lizzy and saying, 'I'm pretty sure the Lord might be calling us to plant a church here.'

Then George W. Bush changed the visa laws.

We couldn't apply for a working visa unless the church had a registered address, established congregation, charity number and all sorts of other things that church plants don't have.

But back in the UK the Lord was working behind the scenes. A bishop was talking to some friends of ours who led a local church in Stockport. In the next-door parish there was an area of high deprivation, which had no gospel presence. Would they consider planting there? So, after what might be best described as 'discernment turbulence' where we grappled with the possibility that the Lord was not, actually, calling us to Southern California but to Stockport, we moved back to the UK and were licensed to plant a church.

We'd gone from being dreamers to doers.

Finding the Meta-Principles

We spent a year building team, creating culture for our new little church, and connecting with people who lived locally. I researched the history of the area, and we looked into the deprivation statistics to consider what issues affected the lives of those who lived there.

As we began this work, the bishop asked us if we would share what we were learning more widely. We put on a conference and fifty people came. It seemed there was an itch that people wanted to scratch. I wondered whether a learning community model might benefit other pioneers and planters.[2] So I thought really hard and came up with a name: 'Pioneer and Planter Days'.

We hosted these learning communities four times a year over a period of four years, each time asking participants to think beyond what was going on, or what activities they were doing, but instead to reflect on what principles were at work in their context.

I love principles. I love the idea that you can take something complex and boil it down to a simple principle. I love the simplicity of $E=mc^2$ (even though I couldn't tell you anything about how Einstein got there). I love business books like Jim Collins' *Good to Great*, which simplifies complex data into foundational tools for leadership.[3]

Back to the Pioneer and Planter Days. The central funding body of the Church of England agreed to fund us as we did this work, and a brilliant woman called Jenny helped to compile what we were doing and turned it into something useable. Every time we gathered we got more principles from the pioneers and planters. One day I asked Jenny, 'Do you think there are some meta-principles?'

Wouldn't that be awesome? Principles that work for any context, whether you're working with deprived children or wealthy young adults? Ageing retirees or broken families? Jenny said she'd take a look. And she gathered every single principle, every comment made, and tried to make some sense of them.

They seemed to fit into two categories.

The first was stuff to do with the leaders, who they needed to *be* – maintaining their own personal prayer life, having and holding a vision, being willing to grow in character, taking initiative and learning from what was going on around them.

The second was stuff they needed to *do* – building a team, connecting with the community, sharing the good news of Jesus, working out a rhythm of community life and worship, and looking beyond themselves to multiply.

She said, 'It's a bit like stones and ripples. You need a stone to make the ripples. And the ripples flow out from the centre.'

Genius.

So we tried to boil the principles down into simple, named categories, to be a reference point for the pioneer. We got it down to five characteristics and five steps. Ten things to remember. Ten principles that can help a pioneer or planter take a step back and consider what's going on, both within themselves as a leader and within what they are leading.

That's my story.

Let's be honest: I don't know your story or background. I don't know what experiences – good or bad – you've had in pioneering or planting something new.

You may be looking for something that might help give a little structure to the planting and pioneering journey. Or you may be thinking, 'I'm not in church leadership' or 'I'm too young' or 'My church would never support something new.' You might have a whole bunch of good reasons that cause you to be frustrated in your dreaming or you might be in the midst of a church plant, and it's not going the way you'd planned.

A Travel Guide

My hope is that you can read through these principles and gain some confidence for the journey ahead. The aim is for this to be a rough guide, a book to read through and then jump back to. I hope you make lots of notes and underline lots of words.

A while back, Lizzy and I went to Greece on holiday.

Just the two of us.

I know.

Before we went, I got some travel guides and read about the area we were going to. It was really interesting and gave me a good idea of the town and what to expect. I clicked open Google Maps and used Street View to see what roads went where and how to get to the apartment. I looked online at the bus timetable and the location of the bus stop.

This meant that by the time we got there, I felt like I knew a little about the place. I had imagined it, planned it, and once we were actually there, we could enjoy the sites, smells and sounds. We had a good idea of what to expect because we had taken the time to read the travel guides.

When we were there, we used more travel guides to help us plan our time. We went for a walk recommended in one guide. We went to a beach we would never have discovered unless we had read about it.

And now we've returned, we can look back at the travel guide. The information which was new to me before is now familiar. I know that place; I've been there.

That's my hope for this book. That you'll read it and get a bit of an idea of the pioneering and planting journey. That you'll come back to it when you need to, as something of a reference guide. And I hope that one day you'll read it and think, yep, that's familiar territory for me now too.

So, these ten things.

Five Characteristics

There are five characteristics of a leader. I'm sure there are probably more, but honestly, when you read through the five, you'll think it's quite enough.

These characteristics are less about what you need to do and more about how to be. They are active words, but they continually challenge me in my relationship with Jesus and help me take responsibility rather than try to blame everyone and everything else when things are tough.

The first is *praying*. Every time we gathered pioneers and planters together this principle came out. It's so easy to forget. It's easy for it to get pushed out because we're so busy for Jesus we don't ever spend any time with him. So, pray – but how? What does it look like to develop a healthy prayer life; seeking God and being led by him as we pioneer and plant?

Second is *envisioning*. How do we get vision? How do we communicate it with others? What is God stirring within our hearts for a particular place or people group?

Third, *growing*. How do we respond to the frustrations we encounter in pioneering and planting? How can we grow in our emotional health? How can we prioritise and set healthy boundaries, to make space for growth? I long to be considered by the Lord as 'mature' in my faith, and the only way that's going to happen is by me growing as a person, as a leader, as a husband, as a dad. (I don't want to be one of those people who establish a great church, but my kids suffer as a result. Lord, no.) So I need to grow. I'm thinking you do too. Well, let's grow together.

Fourth, *acting*. The one thing I don't want the Lord to consider me is a hypocrite, saying one thing and doing another. (I'm guessing you're the same.) Or worse, saying one thing and not doing anything at all. Dreamers who spend their whole life dreaming, but never reaching for the goal, end up sad, depressed and disappointed. What's the balance between getting on with things and waiting for God to do something?

Fifth, *learning*. What are the ways we can learn about our context, our people, our mission, our strategies? How do we embrace the change that inevitably comes about?

I'd like to suggest that if we work on these five characteristics, we'll be leaders that others might want to follow, pioneers that might see a breakthrough. We'll model a life that others might want to live; an example of discipleship which is wholehearted, humble, passionate and sees lives transformed in Jesus' name.

Those are the five characteristics. What about the five steps to take us from vision to multiplication?

Five Steps

First, *leading*. How do we lead others? Leadership means influence, and we want our influence to be positive. Leaders set the culture. Leading exposes our weaknesses, so it's important that we know how to be emotionally healthy, so that what flows into those around us is for good. *Prayer* starts in the leaders and flows out; the leaders are the *vision* carriers; the leaders are constantly striving to *grow* and set a culture of discipleship ... See how the ripples come out from the leader to those around them? You get the idea.

Second, *relating*. Pioneering and planting is about people, and sharing the good news of Jesus with people means relationships. But how do we balance our relationships with those who join us to fulfil the vision and our relationships with those we are trying to reach? And what about our relationships with the organisations who might be supporting or working alongside us?

Third, *incarnating*. This is where most people think planting and pioneering begins – starting a new project, creating a new community, beginning a work that demonstrates the love and life of God with new people. What are the principles behind demonstrating the kingdom of God in 'carne' – in the flesh?

Fourth, *establishing*. Honestly, this tends to be the bit where most pioneers can get bored. Pioneers can become fixated on the new, the exciting. Establishing is about creating the trellis around which the plant can grow – the structures, the systems, the shape of the community. Without it, like any human community void of structure, it will tend to collapse. For something to survive and thrive, it needs a framework.

What are the healthy structures we can build to help establish and sustain things beyond our limited presence?

Fifth, *multiplying*. Healthy parents want their children to grow to the point that they are ready to leave home. How can we invest in a leadership pipeline, developing other pioneers and planters to initiate something new themselves?

These are our ten principles. We'll look at each one in turn, taking some stories from Scripture and from our experience of pioneering and planting. I hope you'll be able to add your own. And that you'll come back to this again and again, to check where you're up to, both within yourself and what you're pioneering.

A few years after planting Glo Church, I was asked by New Wine England, a network of church leaders who gather with their churches and twenty thousand other Christians every summer, to raise the profile of church planting. So I started sharing these principles through the New Wine family.

Lizzy, the kids and I then moved to plant the first resource church in Greater Manchester (the first in the north of England, by about a day).[4] There's more on that story later. The reason I mention it is because these principles have helped us as we planted there too.

Principles to keep us focused on being who God has called us to be. And principles to help us navigate the journey as we lead others on it.

Let's get into it.

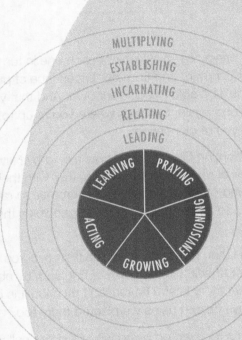

SECTION ONE

ST●NES

Have you ever watched what happens when you throw a stone into a pond?

First, you get a really satisfying 'plop' sound, as the stone hits the water and becomes engulfed. Second, the plop creates ripples that flow outwards from the very place the stone entered the water.

The stone creates the ripples – no stone, no ripples. And the stone is *all in*: no going back.

The letter to the Hebrews describes Jesus as a *pioneer*, one who began something new.[1] Talk about someone who was all in!

Although a stone being thrown into a pond might not be the perfect analogy of Jesus being sent to earth, or us being sent into the mission field (for a start, the stone is inanimate, and by the fact you're reading this, you're not), I think it helps capture the image of someone being thrown into a new environment and impacting that place for good.

Jesus gave up the glory of heaven to enter the mess of humanity. The first chapter of John's Gospel tries to grapple with how this worked – Jesus is fully God and fully human, and also somehow pre-existent: 'In the beginning was the Word, and the Word was with God, and the Word was God. He was with God in the beginning.'[2]

Jesus was sent from heavenly glory by the Father to broken humanity, like a stone thrown from perfection into a dirty pond, whose ripples continue to this day.

From 'Holy!' to 'Crucify!'

Let's consider that heavenly glory Jesus left as he threw himself 'all in' to rescue us. To do this, we need a quick theology check on heaven – we're not talking about babies with wings or angels on clouds with harps (that was just our medieval friends trying to get their head around the word 'glory').

Heaven is the realm of God's rule and reign, where what he wants happens.

This is what Jesus left – a place where he was constantly honoured for who he is and what he has done. He swapped the perfection of heaven for the brokenness of humanity, and was honoured by a few but questioned by many – including his own family.

Early in Jesus' ministry, his family came along to take him home, clearly embarrassed by what was happening. They explained his actions by saying, 'He is out of his mind.'[3] It's easy to imagine them awkwardly apologising to their neighbours and friends.

What?! The angels in heaven worship him as holy,[4] but his family tried to shut him up and take him home so people would stop talking about them ...

Eventually, in place of 'holy, holy' comes 'crucify, crucify'. Jesus became completely engulfed in the brokenness of humanity, precisely so he could set us free from it.

All In

Jesus went from a place of supreme glory to being a baby, trapped in the space-time continuum within human flesh, born in a stable, laid in a manger. For thirty-three years or so, Jesus was limited, just as we are, by his own flesh. At times, he didn't even have a place to lay his head.[5]

Jesus was willing to give up all that glory, so that we could know freedom, and share the glory with him.

Paul puts it like this in Philippians, quoting the song that the church had begun to sing about Jesus, the one who gave up everything for us:

> God,
> did not consider equality with God something to be
>   used to his own advantage;
> rather, he made himself nothing
> by taking the very nature of a servant,
> being made in human likeness.
> And being found in appearance as a man,
> he humbled himself
> by becoming obedient to death –
> even death on a cross!
>
> Therefore God exalted him to the highest place
> and gave him the name that is above every name,
> that at the name of Jesus every knee should bow,
> in heaven and on earth and under the earth,
> and every tongue acknowledge that Jesus Christ is Lord,
> to the glory of God the Father.[6]

Here's the point: Jesus was *all in*.

Pioneering and planting is demanding. We are thrown into new contexts, new relationships, new environments, facing new challenges, new issues, new questions. We deal with things we never expected. But, like Jesus, we do it for the sake of others. Not for our own advantage, success or vanity. But that others might know the good news of Jesus, and that he might get the glory.

The verse from Hebrews – the one I mentioned earlier that speaks of Jesus as a pioneer – reminds us that he endured the cross for the joy set before him.[7] The prize was worth the price. And it goes on to encourage us in the midst of our challenges: 'Consider him who endured such opposition from sinners, so that you will not grow weary and lose heart.'[8]

Being 'all in' doesn't protect us from opposition, and it's hard to be obedient if we're only partially committed to something.

I wonder how you're feeling right now. Are you fully committed? What might it look like for you to be 'all in' to the mission God is calling you into? What holds you back from letting Jesus have his way in your life? What's the prize you hold on to as you face the cost?

Holiness = Weight

The stone creates the ripples. The bigger the stone, the bigger the impact. The bigger the impact, the bigger the ripples.

The stone is the pioneer – it's you, and those who go with you – starting something new, sent by the Lord and thrown into a new context to see what impact you can make with and for Jesus. It would be easy to think the size of the stone is the size of the team you take, or the amount of money you have behind you as you begin, or the vastness of your vision and dreams.

I'd like to suggest, however, that the size of the stone is related to the *character* of the pioneer.

Think about it. The best pioneer that ever lived, Jesus, was himself the pure, sinless Incarnation (with a capital 'I'). His impact was in proportion to his holiness – being willing to submit himself to God's will and allowing himself to go through the false trial and horrific crucifixion was the very thing that won salvation for us.

Don't get me wrong – I'm not saying you have to be perfect to be a pioneer or planter.

What I mean is that we often get it wrong, looking first at outward things: strategy, team, finances, vision, etc. These things are important, but the Lord is looking for someone he can entrust them to. Someone who will pursue relationship with him in the successes as well as the failures. Someone whose heart is captured by God and who will allow the vision to flow from there. Someone who will prioritise their own holiness above other people's (otherwise they become a hypocrite). Someone who will give things a go, in response to the Lord's nudge. Someone who will keep their eyes open and, if necessary, in humility, change their plans.

In the Old Testament, the glory and holiness of God was experienced as a cloud, as a weight of his presence. I'm suggesting that the greater the holiness, the heavier the weight of God's presence: the heavier the stone, the bigger the impact.

I knew a pioneer – let's call him Aled.

Aled had been a 'successful' pioneer, starting many new initiatives that engaged both de-churched and unchurched people.

Like I said, Aled was a successful pioneer.

And then he had an affair with a woman on his team. He lost his position, his ministry, his influence and his family.

Everything.

All he had worked for fell crumbling to the ground.

Does it mean that everyone who responded to Jesus through his work is now invalidated as a disciple? No. Does it mean he can never be restored to ministry and mission? No. Does it mean the works he established have failed? No. Does it mean the things he shared when he trained others were wrong? No.

It just means he got taken out. And a lot of people got hurt in the process. The kingdom of God lost someone who was making an impact in our generation because his immediate desires for a person overcame his commitment to his family, his sense of call, his responsibilities for others.

We all fall short of God's standards of perfection and holiness, so it can't be *that* which discounts us from effective ministry. But here, at the start of our conversation, it's worth considering the thing that's rarely talked about in church-planting and pioneering contexts. Before the strategy and team building and vision and plans, there's *you* (the pioneer), and your relationship with the Lord.

How are you doing in your relationship with Jesus? Are you allowing him into the deepest parts of your life? Are there people around you to whom you can 'confess your sins to each other and pray for each other so that you may be healed'?[9] Throughout Scripture we clearly see that holiness is important to the Lord. Being set apart, consecrated, different, pure ... holiness describes these characteristics. It describes the Lord himself, and what he desires for us.

Pursuing Holiness

John and Charles Wesley, the kingdom pioneers who started the Methodist movement, developed in their early years what they described as 'the holiness code'. A way of living which would keep them holy. However, they both struggled with the reality that they couldn't do it themselves. They couldn't achieve a works-based righteousness.

John came to realise that he'd got it all wrong, and that righteousness came through faith in Christ. As he gathered with Moravian Christians and they worshipped together, he was baptised in the Spirit, his heart was 'strangely warmed', and his ministry was transformed.

Don't think for a second, however, that he lost the desire to pursue holiness and perfection in this life. The whole Methodist movement was a collection of small groups of people who had responded to the good news of Jesus and were trying to work out their lives of faith together.

At the start of each group meeting they would confess their sins to one another from the previous week. If they refused, they had to leave the group until they were willing to be open and honest. After this, they would ask each other questions about how well they had followed Jesus in the previous week, and then they prayed and supported each other to try to live more effectively for Jesus in the following week. They pursued holiness to the very end of life itself, so that by the time people came to the point of death it was like stepping through a thin curtain from this life to the next: close to Jesus and worshipping him in this life, and doing the very same thing the moment after their very last breath.

John Wesley called it 'dying well'.

Remember, we're not called to perfection in everything. We're called to relentlessly pursue holiness. And in Scripture, we see that holiness is a really big deal to the Lord.

Just as he is holy: set apart, consecrated, different, pure – so he wants his people to be holy too. When the Lord gave Moses the plans for the Tabernacle, the tent of worship, there was to be the 'holy of holies' or the 'most holy place' which was only accessible on one day a year by the high priest, on the Day of Atonement. A whole set of sacrifices had been made to ask forgiveness for those times when the people and the priests had let God, themselves or others down.[10]

Through Moses, God gave the laws, which were a way of demonstrating that this people group were set apart, different to the other nations around them. Moses himself was not allowed to enter the promised land because he 'broke faith' with the Lord and 'did not uphold [the Lord's] holiness'.[11]

Four times through the book of Leviticus – the book of the law – God says, 'Be holy, because I am holy.'[12]

But don't go thinking that this only related to the people under the law, the old covenant. Peter himself quotes this verse in his first letter:

> As obedient children, do not conform to the evil desires you had when you lived in ignorance. But just as he who called you is holy, so be holy in all you do; for it is written: 'Be holy, because I am holy.'[13]

Peter talks about living as if we are foreigners here on earth[14] – Paul describes it as being citizens of heaven[15] – set apart, consecrated, different, pure.

It would seem you and I are called to live life differently. To look different as we live our lives here in the twenty-first century; in the post-industrial, post-Christian, post-modern culture that we call home.

Remember, the bigger the stone, the bigger the impact. The bigger the impact, the bigger the ripples.

Measuring Impact

Jesus was the most holy person to ever live. Tempted in every way, yet without sin.[16] And he had the most significant impact of any human who ever lived. Billions of people follow him; thousands have gone to their deaths over the last two millennia because they trust in him. But think about it: he was a wandering preacher who never spoke in public anywhere beyond a tiny outpost of the Roman Empire. He was executed, and on that day you could count his followers, at most, on two hands.

As Jesus died on the cross, the curtain in the temple was torn in two – the separation between God's holiness and humanity's brokenness had finally been bridged. The final, perfect offering had been made, and God's presence became accessible for anyone who would put their faith in Jesus and his atonement.

A couple of months later, when news began to circulate about his resurrection, there were around one hundred and twenty people who gathered in Jerusalem – a relatively small group of people, set apart for Jesus, choosing to believe this incredible news. Hardly a massive impact.

And yet, because of Jesus' obedience to the will of God, because he chose to be set apart in a way that only he understood at the time, everything changed.

So again: the size of the stone isn't the amount of people you have, or money or vision or dreams or excitement. I'm arguing that the level of impact your pioneering will have is directly proportional to holiness, demonstrated through obedience.

I hope this encourages you in two ways. First, I hope you're encouraged to pursue holiness in a more intentional way. Second, I hope you're encouraged that 'success' isn't always measured in the way the world measures it.

To all intents and purposes, by the end of Jesus' earthly life, it looked like he had failed. Yes, he had ministered to large crowds. Yes, he had done remarkable things, seeing people healed, walking on water, multiplying food for thousands to eat, raising people from the dead. But people were quite happy to see him killed. It's not like people rioted at the verdict to execute him.

However, his obedience is what changed everything for us.

Not perfection, but holiness. Not skills, but obedience.

Our authority in Christ comes from our willingness to be obedient to his kingdom command and commission: '"Love the Lord your God with all your heart and with all your soul and with all your strength and with all your mind"; and, "Love your neighbour as yourself"';[17] and 'go and make disciples of all nations, baptising them in the name of the Father and of the Son and of the Holy Spirit, and teaching them to obey everything I have commanded you'.[18]

The five characteristics we're about to look at are aimed at trying to help consider what it means to be obedient, to be holy, as pioneers.

Lots has been said and written about the 'DNA' of church. But think about it: my kids have Lizzy's and my DNA. In the same way, a new community being pioneered will carry the DNA of the pioneers. To the level *you* pray, your community will pray. Why? Because they will learn it from you. So as we think and dream about the kind of community we hope to see established, we must begin with considering these things within ourselves, so that what we see outworked in our community is coming from a healthy place in us.

Then we will be working in a way that Peter envisioned, as 'a chosen people, a royal priesthood, a holy nation, God's special possession, that you may declare the praises of him who called you out of darkness into his wonderful light'.[19]

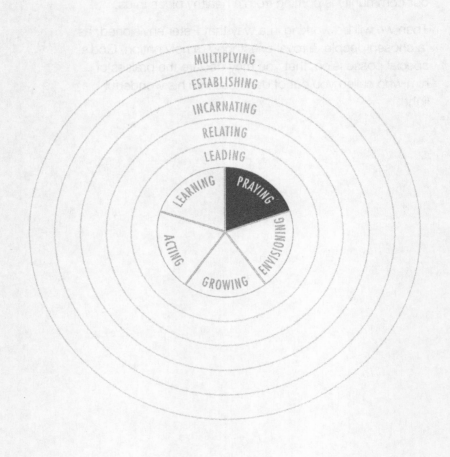

1

Praying

Four times a year, for four years, we gathered pioneers together in the centre of Manchester and asked them: what principles are at work in your context? Based on the things that are going well and based on the things you wish were going better, what principles can you determine?

I've always been interested in principles. I love asking, 'Why?' Because of this, I fell in love with physics when doing my GCSEs, because it got into the 'why' of things. I decided to study it at A-Level, which is a bit of a shame, as I didn't clock quite how much maths was involved! But my motive was the same.

I wanted to know *why*.

With pioneering and planting, I wanted to know why some things worked and some didn't, and the leaders who gathered with us found it helpful to reflect on this as well. We decided to engage with the process of what theologians call 'reflective practice': taking a moment to step back, process what's currently going on, consider what can be learned from what's gone before and what you could have done differently – and crucially, what you are going to do moving forward.

So we gathered a number of pioneers. We had some good coffee (obviously). We spent some time together in worship. We reflected on our current contexts and the principles at work there. Then we shared together, writing down our principles on sticky notes and plastering them around the room.

Between us, we wrote down hundreds of principles, all of which helped form the concept of stones and ripples. Some principles cropped up regularly and became an obvious theme for planting. Others were only noted once – a principle crucial for that moment in time, but specific to an individual place, project or person.

But every time we gathered, there was one reoccurring principle, written on multiple sticky notes by a number of people:

Prayer.

It seems obvious, but every time we got together, we needed to remind ourselves that prayer was foundational to everything we were doing.

We discovered it's really easy to put a lot of thought and effort into the pressing needs of those around us. A few of us, including Lizzy and me, were working in deprived areas, and the needs of the people we were working with could be particularly challenging. Our attention was often focused on how to support, nurture, encourage and disciple those who were on a journey of faith, while also dealing with complex situations and backgrounds.

For others in the group, the pressing need was the projects they were running: building the team, connecting with other agencies, raising funds and working out the next steps as things developed.

Sometimes the need was sustaining the structures that had been established: trying to get the balance between encouraging teams to be missional, while also addressing pastoral needs, or raising up other volunteers to join the work, either from within the context or beyond.

And every time, we realised how prayer was crucial to the breakthrough in all of these things. It became a bit of a running joke. How could we have forgotten? Why isn't prayer the first thing we try, instead of – at times – the last?

It All Starts with Prayer

Prayer is the foundation of any relationship with God. It's obvious when you think about it – you can't have a *relationship* unless you *relate* to someone. So, in order to develop our relationship with God, prayer is vital.

Archbishop John Sentamu has said, 'No Christian is greater than their prayer life.'[1]

Prayer is important and foundational, but we're not the only ones to get on with the mission and then realise we need the foundation of prayer to sustain us. Jesus' own disciples asked him, 'Lord, teach us to pray.'[2] But this was *after* he sent them out to preach the kingdom, heal the sick and drive out demons. So what can we learn from Jesus about how we might deepen our life of prayer?

Jesus often sought time alone to pray. For important decisions he did a lot of praying.

Early in his ministry, a big decision was weighing down on him. There was a growing number of people following him, and he wanted to develop a core group of twelve disciples who could take on responsibilities and share the mission with him. But who to choose?

He 'often withdrew to lonely places and prayed'[3] and for this decision, he wanted to get away, to be with the Father, to ask and to listen.

Presumably he told some of the key disciples around him what he was planning and that he needed to be alone. Most likely some of the people he told were the ones he had in mind to choose as his team.

As usual, crowds would be gathering around him in the hope that he might heal them or the person they were with, or that they might hear some of his teaching. Perhaps he packed up early before the crowds reached him, or maybe he withdrew from them before the sun went down.

Then off he went. Up a mountainside.

There he prayed, all night.

Asking and listening.

As we reflected on prayer in our pioneer gatherings, we began to see that it fell into two different roles of *asking* and *listening*. A bit like *breathing out* and *breathing in*. Bringing our requests and waiting for an answer. Asking for help and seeking wisdom for what to do. Breathing out and breathing in.

Just as breathing is vital for sustaining life itself, so asking and listening prayer are vital for sustaining the faith life of both the pioneer and their work.

Let's take a look at each.

Asking Prayer

Hannah was miserable. Her husband loved her and treated her well, but she was on the receiving end of abuse from someone else in the family: her husband's other woman. (Yep, I'm meaning the Hannah in 1 Samuel, at a time when polygamy was normal.[4])

Your status as a woman in this heavily patriarchal society was determined by your child-bearing abilities and often by how many children you had produced. Amazingly, her husband didn't seem bothered – he loved her and told her not to worry about it – but Peninnah, her rival, mocked her until she cried. This went on for years. Because of the abuse, at times, Hannah refused to eat.

Hannah went to the Lord about her troubles. (Even then she was misunderstood, with Eli the priest wrongly concluding she was drunk because of the way she was praying.)

She was praying out of her 'deep anguish', 'weeping bitterly' before the Lord.[5] Sometimes it's good just to get it all out.

'Lord, help.'

A passionate request.

There have been times when Lizzy and I have been pioneering something new, and I've found myself alone, on the floor, lying face down, in deep anguish – and once or twice weeping bitterly – asking for the Lord's help.

'Lord, this is too hard. Lord, I can't go on. Lord, bring the breakthrough. Lord, people are saying untrue things about us. Lord, I'm being misinterpreted. Lord, I think I made a mistake. Lord, why are they still not healed? Lord, please provide.'

'Lord, help.'

Paul encourages the Ephesian church to 'pray in the Spirit on all occasions with all kinds of prayers and requests. With this in mind, be alert and always keep on praying for all the Lord's people.'[6] He adds colour to this when writing to the Philippians, saying 'in every situation, by prayer and petition, with thanksgiving, present your requests to God'.[7]

On all occasions ... in every situation ... be alert ... always keep on praying ...

Whether things are going just as we'd hoped or as bad as could be, pray. To encourage us in this, think of all the parts of the Lord's Prayer that are requests:

Hallowed be your name (may your name be honoured) ...

Your kingdom come, your will be done, on earth as it is in heaven (let what you want happen) ...

Give us today our daily bread (give us all we need to survive and thrive) ...

Forgive us our debts (we're sorry, please wipe the slate clean) ...

Lead us not into temptation (keep us from unnecessary trials and tribulations) ...

Deliver us from the evil one (don't let the accuser have his way in us or with us).[8]

The prayer translates from Greek into fifty English words, and only twelve are not requests. Asking God accounts for 74 per cent of the prayer. The rest is worship, or relates to us committing to forgive others.

It's become my practice each morning to go through the Lord's Prayer, line by line, letting the Holy Spirit guide me to situations that connect with each theme within the prayer. Asking the Lord, using the prayer he gave us.

I begin praying in tongues, allowing my spirit to connect with the Holy Spirit, and worshipping the Lord. Then I thank God that he is my Father, that in Jesus I am adopted into his family and that I have the Holy Spirit within, as the deposit, guaranteeing what is to come. I also remember he is 'our' Father – Father of *all* humanity, as well as adoptive Father of *all* who call on Jesus (even the ones I disagree or struggle with …). Then I pray that he would be honoured in my life, in our church and in our world, worshipping him for all the ways he is good, holy and pure.

I then think through all the places in my life, our church and the world where I long to see his kingdom come and his will being done – for healing, breakthrough, good relationships, for those in need, for my family and friends, for the government and those in authority. I let my thoughts wander over things and trust the Holy Spirit is bringing to mind what I need to pray for. Here, I also try to pray for those people to whom I've said, 'I'll pray for you.'

Then I pray for provision: spiritually, physically, mentally, emotionally and financially. 'Lord, please give me what I need today. Lord, please provide for us as a church; give us what we need, not just to survive but thrive.'

I then take time to forgive others – choosing to set people free from my judgement or frustrations – and ask God's forgiveness of me.

After this I ask God's protection over me, my family, my church, our world – that we would not have to go through very difficult times and that the strategies of the enemy would not flourish but wither; that what he works for evil, God will turn for good. That anxiety would become anxious due to the victory of Jesus, that fear would become afraid … that the accuser would be the one who is frustrated, as his plans turn to nothing other than the glory of God in Jesus.

We can sometimes wonder whether we are praying in line with God's

will. Praying the Lord's Prayer is a great way of knowing that we are.
Jesus literally told us to pray this stuff. So when we pray this prayer,
we know the Father hears us. We come to him through Jesus, in the
presence and power of the Holy Spirit, with great humility, and pray. I'm
not saying this gets us everything we ask for. I'm saying it helps us be
confident that the Father hears us.

Jesus said that 'everyone who asks receives'.[9] 'Asks' here is in the
present imperative tense – ask and keep on asking. Seek: keep looking
and working for the answer. Knock: keep persisting in prayer.

Then he reminds his listeners about the nature of the Father, which is
to give good gifts to his children – including, as Luke tells it, the gift of
the Holy Spirit.[10]

Later, Jesus told his disciples the parable of the persistent widow, to
urge them to pray and never give up. The widow continues banging on
the door of the judge for her case to be heard. 'And will not God bring
about justice for his chosen ones, who cry out to him day and night?'[11]

It seems we're being encouraged to harass God with our prayers and
requests.

The Scriptures use the word 'intercession' to describe this kind of
prayer.[12] The Latin word *intercedere* literally means 'to go between'.[13] To
bridge between one thing and another: let 'your kingdom come … on
earth as it is in heaven'. This is why we can feel tension in prayer – we
are bridging the gap; holding on to the promises of God in the midst of
a reality that doesn't reflect it.

Jesus is interceding for us too.[14] And the Holy Spirit helps us,
sometimes just with 'wordless groans'.[15] That's been so comforting to
me – sometimes I just run out of words, and groans are the best way
to sum it up. Sometimes, using the gift of tongues is the best way to let
our spirits pray. Other times, a good 'ugh' does the trick. 'Lord, I have
no idea what to do. Lord, this is tough.'

'Lord, help.'

You can ask God for help, for wisdom, for provision, for peace – for the
things you need. And you can ask God for the things your community

needs too. Jesus is inviting – encouraging! – you to ask, and keep on asking.

Sometimes there's an unexpected answer. Whenever Lizzy and I have stepped out into something new, God has done something significant in answer to a prayer, giving us the encouragement that he is at work, and growing our faith in him. I've begun to look for what I now call an 'apostolic miracle' when I first arrive in a new place. One time, I was getting to know someone after we'd just moved to a different city; she had broken her foot and was wearing a cast, so I offered to pray for it. I didn't think much of it, but when I saw her next, she explained she had been healed, and the cast had been taken off. Amazing! And I didn't even really pray with that much faith! It was just a demonstration of God's abundant goodness. An 'apostolic miracle' to encourage me that God was on the move in that place.

Then there are the long-term prayers, praying for chronic physical or mental illnesses, for cancer, for people in palliative care. We try to pray in a way that leaves the person feeling loved rather than feeling they have a lack of faith if nothing happens in the moment. We pray 'your kingdom come today' and commit to praying that prayer until it's answered – either through a miracle, or on that great and glorious day when we meet with Jesus and are transformed into his likeness.

So in all sorts of ways we ask God, trusting in his goodness, for people to be healed, set free from unhealthy spirits, for provision, for breakthrough, for things to turn out his way.

We bridge the gap between our reality and God's reality. We keep bringing our needs, and the needs of our community, to him, and ask: 'Lord, help.'

Listening Prayer

If prayer is like breathing, then listening is just as important as asking. If breathing out is asking prayer, then breathing in – getting the oxygen, the fuel we need to keep going – is listening prayer.

In Acts 16, Paul and some friends were out on mission in the middle of Turkey – what was then called Phrygia and Galatia. They began to travel north-west and came to two borders – going west into Mysia or north into Bithynia. They tried to go north 'but the Spirit of Jesus would not allow them to'.[16]

I'd love to know more details about what this looked like. There's no record of a prophetic word or heavenly sign saying, 'Not this way.' There's no angel appearing, no voice from above. Most likely it was a 'sense' that some of them had. It might have been as simple as some kind of border control that they later interpreted as guidance. But my guess is it was a simple lack of peace.

Paul wrote to the Colossians, 'Let the peace of Christ rule in your hearts.'[17] The word 'rule' in this context means 'referee'.

When the ref blows the whistle, the game stops. Something's not right. Either someone is injured or something has happened to bring the game to a halt. The ball went out of bounds. A foul occurred. The time has run out.

The peace of Christ functions like the ref's whistle. Or rather, the lack of peace is like the whistle has blown, and our attention turns to the Lord.

Paul exhorts the church in Colossae not just to a personal peace, but to corporate peace, 'as members of one body you were called to peace'.[18] When Paul gave this advice, maybe he had in mind the trip recorded in Acts 16, where *together*, they sensed a lack of peace about Bithynia:

It just doesn't seem right. OK, let's go west instead.

So they went through Mysia towards Troas, a journey of about two hundred and fifty miles. You'd want to be sure you'd got that decision right, especially if you were walking!

And there, in Troas, Paul had a dream of a Macedonian man asking him to come and help.[19] Paul and his friends took that to be a sign from the Lord, and off they went to Philippi, a key city in Macedonia, and planted a church there.

When he was Archbishop of Canterbury, Rowan Williams said that mission is 'finding out what God is doing and joining in'.[20] This seems a good description of what Paul and his friends were up to in Turkey, and what we get up to in listening prayer.

Listening to God is discerning what he's doing and what he's saying. Jesus said that he only did what he saw the Father doing.[21]

If this was true of Jesus, then we should endeavour to make it true of ourselves.

Learning to look with eyes of faith, learning to have one ear tuned to what people are saying and another ear tuned to the whisper of the Spirit. Judging our gut reactions through the peace of Christ.

Of course, to grow in discernment requires absorbing God's Word. We need to be people who are reading Scripture and reflecting on how biblical principles might be transferable to our current context. As Karl Barth said, 'Take the Bible in one hand and the daily newspaper in the other'.[22] Know the Scriptures, and know your current context.

Paul recognised the importance of the Word in helping us be guided by peace. In his letter to the Colossians, he connects the *peace* of Christ with the *message* of Christ:

> Let the peace of Christ rule in your hearts, since as members of one body you were called to peace. And be thankful. Let the message of Christ dwell among you richly as you teach and admonish one another with all wisdom through psalms, hymns, and songs from the Spirit, singing to God with gratitude in your hearts.[23]

Reading Scripture, talking it through with others and absorbing it during corporate worship are all part of learning what it means to grow in discernment.

When Lizzy and I were invited to consider moving to Salford in central Manchester, we felt an initial sense of excitement and sensed the call of God. We knew that moving from the church we had planted six years previously would be costly, but we also believed there was something fresh for us on the horizon.

I decided to do a prayer walk in Salford, to get a sense of the area and to try to listen to the whisper and nudge of the Spirit. I asked one of the bishops involved in the invitation process to give me the name of the church and then searched for it online before heading there physically. We had been asked to plant a 'resource church' – a church plant that would plant other churches – just by the city centre and next to Salford University.

When I arrived at the church building, I began to have concerns. I had a bizarre sense of peace about the call to plant, but no peace about the specifics. The church wasn't located near the city centre or the university, and the transport links didn't make sense either. I prayed all around the building and just couldn't work it out. Something wasn't quite right. I didn't have peace.

I decided to walk from the church building into the centre of Manchester and find Salford University. I put it into my phone and followed the directions – including a two-lane highway with no pathway. I kept thinking, *How are people going to get to this church from the university?* I still had a sense of peace about the overall call, but none about the details.

I walked for about half an hour and came towards a train station, finally seeing some other people walking around – *thank goodness*, I thought. I saw the university and began to do some research about where those students lived. I went into a local estate agents and asked the staff, 'If I were to buy a student house as an investment, would I buy it near to the church I've just walked from?'

'No.'

Hmm.

I hadn't seen another church building for the entire time I'd been walking.

Lord, what's going on?

I stepped out of the estate agency shopfront and stood still for a moment, totally confused. I had what can only be described as a prayer-gut-reaction: it was both a conviction and a prayer at the same time, a sense of heavenly rightness along with my own desire and request.

Lord, if only there was a church here, *this would be the perfect place to plant.*

I looked up and saw a church building just down the road. No way! With my attention focused on the building and faith rising, I walked quickly towards it.

It turned out to be the Catholic cathedral.

I walked into the city centre, wandered around continuing my prayer walk for the people there, and asking for wisdom and discernment about our call.

I drove home and chatted about it with Lizzy. We both sensed the same: God's peace about the general call, but concern about key elements.

So I texted the bishop: 'We sense it's right, but we have some concerns about the location.'

I got the reply pretty quickly. 'Sorry, wrong church! I meant this one' – and he sent me a link to the website.

I clicked the link and laughed out loud when I saw where the church was – just where I had prayed, 'God *this* would be the perfect place.' I later returned to the same spot to try to work out how I'd missed the church and realised a building obstructs the view to Saint Philips Chapel Street.

I saw in my spirit what I couldn't see in the physical. God's peace filled Lizzy and me when we prayed that night; we went to bed laughing with joy and with the most amazing heavenly fragrance filling our room.

Let the peace of God rule in your hearts.

We shared the details of the resource church with a few trusted friends, who prayed with us and for us, and as we talked it through with them it seemed to confirm the sense of call.

We took our kids to prayer walk around the (correct) church, knowing the decision would impact them, and they too got a sense of excitement about it. In the city centre we went into a Starbucks where they were playing the track, 'Good Good Father'.[24] Never before nor since have we heard a Christian song being played in a Starbucks. But at that moment, as we were praying for peace about a key decision in the life of our family, they were playing a song that spoke deeply to us.

Listening prayer helped us make the decision to say yes; it helped discern the mind of Christ for our next steps.

How do you listen to God? Maybe you're not even sure you'd recognise the voice of God if you heard it. But peace is like the 'gentle whisper' that God used to speak to Elijah in 1 Kings.[25] In that passage, the Hebrew text doesn't mention a voice, just a gentle sound of stillness, silence or calm.

You don't need to hear God's audible voice to listen to him, but when you're trying to discern God's leading, get some people around you, get into the Word, and listen for the gentle sound of calm.

The Practice of Prayer

It's also important that we keep prayer going beyond just the significant moments in life. If reading the Scriptures helps us learn more about the nature of God, and if prayer and worship help us engage with God, then establishing prayer as a regular practice in our own lives is absolutely essential if we want to see prayer develop in the communities we plant.

As pioneers we need to establish a habit of prayer and Bible study as a recurring practice, to help nurture and sustain us. This habit, over time, then impacts the rhythm and faith life of the growing community.

When we first planted in Stockport, I used to worship and pray each morning. Lizzy was off on the school run, and we were trying to discern what steps to take in our new area. We had many things we were asking the Lord about: team, vision, people's needs, our own family challenges.

So I took on the practice I had seen in a church I'd previously worked in: worship and prayer at 9 a.m. Historically, this has been known as the 'daily office' – a time set aside to pray, worship and read Scripture in the morning and evening. I didn't know that then; I just thought it would be a good practice for the future, as it had served us well in the past.

Like most of us, I had my own time with the Lord, reading Scripture and in prayer before the day really got going, but my time at 9 a.m. was more focused around the church and the community we were seeking to establish. In time, as more people joined the team, we ended up with a staff, including paid and volunteer members, and we prayed every weekday morning together.

A friend of mine makes sure he prays Compline every night before bed.[26] His wife finds it amusing, but he finds the Lord in the space that the words and prayers create.

Last autumn we were launching Alpha, and the central office suggested praying for three people every day for three weeks, by setting an alarm at 10.02. Why then? Because Luke 10:2 is the verse where Jesus encourages his disciples to pray for mission in the harvest field.

How could you develop a practice of prayer for yourself and your community? If it's a geographical community, gathering regularly can be really helpful. If it's a demographic community spread over a wide area, technology can help – a WhatsApp group text at a regular time each day is one example. What would help you? What would help your community?

What's in us as pioneers flows out of us. And our pioneering begins and ends with prayer.

Our prayers include both asking and listening: coming to God with our requests and interceding for others, along with discerning what he might be saying and where he might be leading us. Breathing out, and breathing in.

May our prayer lives become like breathing. We can't survive without it.

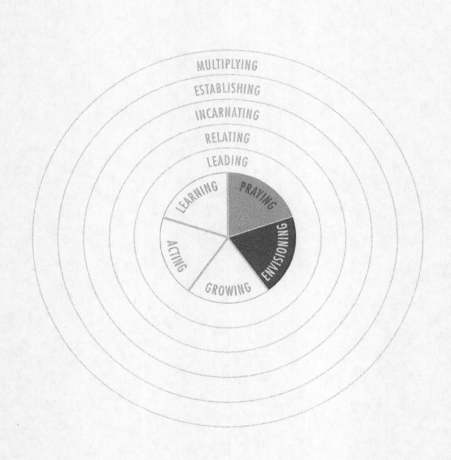

2

Envisioning

Everything new begins with vision. Seeing something beyond what currently exists, and going for it.

When we first planted Saint Philips Chapel Street, there were twenty-three of us, including nine children. The building itself was originally designed two centuries ago for 1,800 people; fire regulations nowadays mean we can squeeze in 'only' about 700. It's a vast Georgian preaching house, built to allow many people to come and hear the good news of Jesus.

So our initial gatherings for worship didn't exactly fill the church ...

However, we dreamed with our team, and those who began to gather with us, about what things would look like when we had grown to a much bigger size.

A few weeks in, we were excited to meet a young woman who had moved to study after completing a gap year with global movement YWAM (Youth With A Mission). At the end of our worship gathering I chatted with her about the vision of the church and what we hoped the Lord would do in and through us. Lizzy had a similar conversation. We came home buzzing, excited about the role she might be able to play in our journey.

Next week she didn't come to worship. We asked her friend if she was OK. Her answer took me aback: she enjoyed it, but she just couldn't see it.

She couldn't *see* it.

In my mind, I could see the chairs beginning to fill up with people who have heard about Jesus, hungry to worship him. I could see a time when the heating would work, we would have a full worship team, groups for kids and young people, outreach and midweek groups going on, all having an impact in the city. But she just couldn't picture it.

What do you long to see?

Our culture is obsessed with the idea that we should chase our dreams. I believe it's in our God-given nature for humans to be creative and imaginative, able to envision something beyond ourselves and work towards it. That, in a snapshot, is vision.

As pioneers and planters, our vision is a kingdom-of-God-inspired dream, which captures us with the heart of God for a particular city or community, to see it transformed in the name of Jesus.

Your kingdom come, your will be done, on earth as it is in heaven.

Our God has vision: out of nothing he pulled together the heavens and the earth. When humanity declined Plan A, God had vision for how it might be resolved: establishing a nation to demonstrate to the rest of humanity what it looks like to live under his rule and reign.

When that didn't go to plan, he had vision for calling that nation back to himself: judges, kings, prophets, finally leading to exile and the remnant.

And then God-in-flesh: to not only show humanity how to live life as it was meant to be – fully engaged with the Father and the Holy Spirit – but also to submit himself to an unjust death, taking upon himself the punishment we deserved.[1]

After that, the real visionary moment, the deal-breaker, the thing nobody expected: resurrection. By conquering death itself, all of creation is invited to share in the fullness of the kingdom of God.

Missio Dei

This is God on mission. Our mission is just a tiny part of this wider mission of God, what theologian David Bosch calls the *missio Dei*.[2] The missionary God, working through his people, enabling them to impact a specific community or people group. Seeing his kingdom come in the here and now, following Jesus as he directs through the prompting of the Holy Spirit.

So although we might have a vision we hold dear ('*my*' vision or '*our*' vision), we must recognise that we are simply sharing a bit of God's vision for our own contexts. This also means we can cheer on other churches and church leaders who are trying to do their bit too.

One of the largest churches in the north-west of England is in Greater Manchester, in Salford. To be more specific, it's a five-minute walk away from us; it's in our parish. They've been nothing but supportive of us as we've planted, and I get on well with the leaders. But it was a little intimidating planting a church with just over twenty people around the corner from a church gathering thousands every Sunday.

A while ago, we got a call asking if they could use our building for a staff team prayer gathering. Sure, we said. The pastor asked if I would share a word with them at the beginning of their time. Sure, I said.

But I remember asking the Lord, 'What do I say?'

'Strengthen, encourage and comfort them.'

These are the key elements of prophecy, according to 1 Corinthians 14:3.

'Speak prophetically to them,' I sensed the Lord say. 'Encourage them in what they are doing.'

As a church, they were about to embark on a very ambitious building project. They were working hard to see God's kingdom come in the city. Our city region has a population of 2.8 million people. Regardless of how big they build their building, it will never serve all the people in Greater Manchester. And even if our building is filled ten times over every Sunday, we'll still only be touching thousands, not even tens of thousands. We need that church, and our church, and every other church in Greater Manchester to dream their biggest dreams, reach for the highest goals, because there are so many people who need to hear about the love of God, shown in Jesus.

Our work fits within the wider context of what God is already doing. And let's be clear: God's vision is not just for my church and your church.

Vision Beyond Church

God certainly does have a vision for the church, but his vision goes way beyond that. So let's not just have a vision for the church we want to establish, but have a vision for the place where the church will grow: the city, town, village or people group where the church will make an impact.

What does God dream for your city or town? What would he love to see happen there? What are the things going on that break his heart? What does he smile over? Having a vision not just for our church, but for the place where we live, means we start to think in terms of God's kingdom, not just our empire or impact.

Nehemiah was gripped with a vision.[3] He served the most powerful ruler of the time and lived a comfortable life,[4] but his spirit was restless. Vision moved him to dare to ask permission from the king to leave his service, move to Jerusalem and rebuild the city walls.

His relationship with God had led him to a place of deep dissatisfaction with how things currently were, and he felt compelled to do something about it.

So, whereas everything starts with vision, vision comes from prayer.

Our asking and listening prayers are the fuel for our vision. For Lizzy and me, our vision for planting a church into the centre of Greater Manchester came through prayer: catching the heart of God, trying to see things from his perspective, wrestling in prayer as the vision became a reality.

Big Vision, Small Steps

Nehemiah had a massive vision. Way, way too big for one man to complete on his own. To see the vision fulfilled he needed permission, money, resources and people. The very same things a pioneer or planter needs. Nehemiah's vision contained two key elements I think we can learn from:

First, it was big enough for people to get excited about.

Nehemiah needed as much help as he could get; there was no way he could rebuild the walls on his own.

Our vision needs to be big enough for people to join in. A compelling vision grabs people and allows them to say, 'I want to be involved in that.' If there's no room for anyone to join in, then guess what? They won't. They might cheer us on, encourage us, support us financially, but they won't join us unless they get a sense they are needed, there's a place for them.

The vision has to have some kind of rallying call – this is what we see, this is what we're aiming for … and you can be a part of it.

When you look around your town or city, what resonates within? What's capturing your heart as you capture God's heart for that area or people group? Does the vision stir you with excitement and passion? If so, it's likely to do the same for others too.

Second, it needs to have small steps so people know what to do. Nehemiah was a genius at this. We are going to rebuild the walls, and this is how we're going to do it.

Vision is great, but in order to fulfil a vision it requires strategy. Strategy involves the steps that need to be taken to see the vision fulfilled. People don't necessarily have to know every part of the strategy before they join in with you, but they do need to know what they can do to help fulfil the vision in the here and now.

Nehemiah called people to rebuild the wall. But then he deployed them at different places around the wall. When attacks came, the strategy changed – everyone was to carry a sword and be ready to gather where the trumpet sounded, to defend the work they were doing. The people who said yes were all in: they captured the vision from Nehemiah and understood what they needed to do to bring it about.

So our vision should be big enough for others to join in, but specific enough so people know what we're asking them to do.

What can people do to help? If someone asked you how they can help, what would you say? If your vision is big enough for others to join in, it must be clear what you want them to do to get involved. Otherwise it might just remain as a great idea that never happens.

So, what's your big vision? What's the thing that stirs your heart and mind, that gets your spirit going? How does it go beyond a new church community and become a blessing that transforms life outside the church building? What words paint the big picture? And what are some of the specifics that people can do to join in? What would someone *do* if they wanted to become part of this vision themselves?

Getting Vision

If you're not quite sure what your answers are to the previous questions, it's worth asking, how do you get vision?

Like with Nehemiah rebuilding the wall, the vision isn't always crystal clear in terms of how to get there, or what it might mean – there's an openness to God doing what he wants, rather than an obsessive control over what we intend. There's also the flexibility to respond to situations when things don't go as planned.

In 2010, Lizzy and I felt God call us to plant a church in Offerton, Stockport. We were living in the US in the months beforehand, so it was hard to prayer walk in Offerton or build much of a team while living across the pond, but we did what we could over the internet. We sensed God in the conversations we had with the church leaders sending us out to plant, but we had never been to the place we were planting. How do you get a vision for that?

We started to pray and research in as many ways as we could. One of my university friends, Paul, grew up in Stockport, and moved back after uni, so I asked him if he could help. He attached his phone to the hands-free holder in his car, and drove around the area narrating what he saw. We looked at maps to try to understand the geography of the place. We used Google's Street View to do some virtual prayer walking around the area.

And we noticed that there didn't seem to be a centre to the town – it was built either side of a main road which had grown, over a couple of hundred years, from a few farms to thousands of homes, but with no centre, no heart.

This became the seed that grew into the big-picture vision: to plant a church on a forgotten social housing estate that would function as the heart of the wider town and community. We would create a social enterprise coffee shop, accessible to all, and offer volunteer and employment opportunities for those looking for a role, putting the profits back into the local community.

We were excited by the vision. It was big, it would have an impact in the community, and it wasn't just church for the sake of church, but church for the sake of others.

We began to share this vision and build team via video calls with a few people. Once we moved to the UK, we researched the area more and made contact with others who might be able to help us fulfil the vision – the owner of the local shopping precinct we hoped to redevelop, the council, other local businesses, funding agencies, and of course the local people.

We shared the vision with all of them.

We took our really small team to look around the shop we hoped to develop. It was grim, with mould everywhere and water running down the walls, but we painted a picture for them of what it could be like. Imagine this here, that there. Imagine people working themselves out of poverty, being a blessing to the local community.

And from that, different people were able to see the specific roles they could play – developing the business plan, kitting out the shop unit, thinking through décor.

Big enough for people to join in (there's no way we could do it on our own) but specific enough for them to know what to do.

They got the vision. We started the work.

And then the owner of the precinct sold it to developers.

We knew this was on the cards, but it had been promised for fourteen years and never happened. We felt we needed to get on with something, so we risked it. We raised a third of the money we needed, but then had no shop front to use.

Sometimes the specifics of the vision don't come to pass. It can be confusing, frustrating – but it drives you back to prayer.

Lord, what's going on? Lord, what are you doing? Lord, help.

A woman from the council who had been supporting us suggested we take a look at another place, right in the centre of the social housing. It had been used as a drop-in centre by the parish council, but they couldn't run it any longer, and wondered if we might like to use it. It wasn't the first time she had offered it, but I had kept turning it down, focused on our vision of a coffee shop.

Lizzy had been saying for a while she thought it was a good idea, but I was not convinced. Reluctantly we agreed to go and look at it.

It was amazing!

It was already fitted out with everything we needed – including a coffee bar area, office space, disabled toilet, and an entire computer suite for people to use. They gave it to us rent-free, and Glo Central was born, our drop-in centre in Offerton. Lizzy ran the centre for five years, and it helped hundreds of people from the local community in multiple ways.

Getting a vision is about capturing the Lord's heart and dream for an area, and partnering with him to see that vision realised.

One Vision, Shared Multiple Ways

Once you're clear on your vision, it will need to be repeated many times, in many contexts, in many ways. I was once encouraged to have a one-minute, five-minute and twenty-minute summary of the vision, so I could share it in detail with those who wanted to hear more, or quickly for those I only met for a moment.

Our vision here in Salford is to be a community which is 'Loving and serving Jesus, each other, Greater Manchester and beyond'. I could talk about that for a minute, or an hour.

What's your vision? Start to hone it into a story that will capture people's hearts, in the same way it has captured yours, and then keep sharing it in lots of different ways.

The vision doesn't need to be perfect – in fact the details will probably change over time. But you're painting an alternative future for people to see: imagine what this place would look like if people were coming to faith in Jesus, and as a result there was reduced crime, stronger families, community cohesion … We would love you to join us and volunteer at our toddler group, as part of what God is doing in this community. The small details and opportunities to serve fit into the wider vision of transformation.

The vision needs to be repeated, in lots of different ways, not just as you're starting out but along the journey too. We have a newcomers' welcome gathering every six weeks or so, to share the vision of the church with the people who have started to worship with us, so they can meet us, and get to hear what we're doing and why we're doing it.

We also remind the church regularly why we do what we do. Otherwise it's easy to forget. For those rebuilding the wall with Nehemiah, all they saw was brick after brick. When they looked to their left, they saw their neighbours building brick after brick. When they looked to their right, the same. Not very inspiring. Nehemiah seemed to keep the big picture in mind when those building the wall couldn't see it, and he kept sharing it with those who were helping in the midst of opposition.[5]

Reminding people of the vision, and telling them how it's going, is key to help them remember why they are doing that particular thing. It may not be very exciting to make and serve coffee, but when it's part of the vision of hospitality, it becomes a way of serving and blessing others, not just putting the kettle on and clearing up cups. Helping with a litter pick is either getting your hands dirty because other people are too lazy to put things in a bin, or a way of blessing your area by making it look more attractive.

You're either stacking bricks, or you're building a wall. Nehemiah kept the vision in mind – not just his own mind, but the mind of the people too.

It's important to not just share the vision of what and why, but also of *how*: this is how we do things here. Setting a culture of how things are done is just as important as sharing the vision of what could be done, and why it should be done. We'll look more into this in the chapter on leading, but just a little note here: Lizzy and I are learning that although people might hear the vision and get excited about it, it doesn't mean they get the culture you're establishing. They can only get that by spending time with you, as you share the why, the what, and demonstrate the how.

Otherwise hospitality does just become serving coffee, and blessing the community is just litter picking. Creating a culture that understands the why and how is about building a team who understand that what they do matters, and the way they do it matters too.

So, if you had thirty seconds, how would you share your vision to someone who's not a Christian? What's the main point you want to put across? Is there anything specific they might be able to do? What about if you're having a meal with someone who is a Christian and is sensing God might be calling them to join you? What's the big picture for them? What are the added details you missed out in your thirty-second presentation? And what could they do to help out?

In all this, the visionary needs to be able to live with the tension that is created between what they see in their spirit and the current reality around them. After all, we live in a kingdom that is both now and not yet. We'll always live in this tension when we are reaching for the establishment of God's kingdom here on earth, as in heaven.

Nehemiah struggled with this too. He went to the Lord with his frustrations, his complaints, and when people were accusing and attacking him.[6]

So, whereas vision starts in prayer, it also drives us back to prayer.

Keep the vision in your mind, keep sharing it with those who have never heard it and those who have heard it dozens of times. Remember why you're doing what you're doing, keep an eye on the culture of how you're getting things done, and help your people remember why they're doing it too.

Keep the vision. Keep sharing the vision.

Keep envisioning.

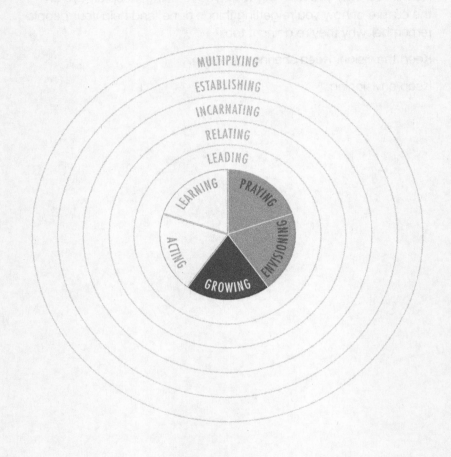

3

Growing

This chapter is not about your church growing. It's about you.

It's about the pioneer growing into maturity; it's about holiness and allowing our struggles not to define us, but grow us.

I'm a perfectionist. I like things done well. I like things to look pleasant, be ordered, make sense, have purpose. In other words, although the Lord might be OK with my limitations, weaknesses and humanity, I'm not so much of a fan.

It can be a pretty stressful place to live.

So I'm growing in becoming more emotionally healthy.

I'm having to learn that, in life, the journey is just as important as the destination. You see, for me, planting a church is about seeing an area transformed, about revival and restoration, about many people bowing the knee to Jesus and finding forgiveness and fullness of life in him; it's about outworking his love in a whole variety of ways. I see the vision really clearly. It excites me.

But I have to remember that I'm human. I have to remember it's the Lord's vision, not mine, and so allow him to use me any way he wants. This includes walking the journey step by step, rather than seeing it all happen by Wednesday and wondering what to do with the weekend.

One season when we were going through a particularly hard time, Lizzy and I took the kids to watch the *Hannah Montana* movie (don't judge me). Our girls were huge fans of the TV series, so we'd got to know the kinds of plot lines we should expect; we were anticipating a pretty saccharine experience. But then, halfway through the film, we had a spiritual encounter right in the middle of the cinema. (It was embarrassing then, and even more so now I'm telling you.) A song got both Lizzy and me sobbing: 'The Climb'.[1] Miley Cyrus belted out this song about uphill battles and wanting mountains to move – the very things we were praying about – but that what matters most is the climb.

Seriously, we were wrecked. We'd been so caught up with the vision, the destination, that we'd forgotten to embrace the journey. We were incredibly stressed about some of the challenges we were facing because it meant we were being slowed down significantly. We had our timetable, our expectations for how it was all meant to work out, and things were not going to plan.

Don't get me wrong; I really do believe we need to keep the end in mind, keep the big picture front and centre so we know where we're going.

But the Lord used *Hannah Montana* to remind us that it's not just the destination that matters, but the journey we take together on the way. He was teaching us how our frustrations can help us grow.

Deborah's Frustrations

In the book of Judges, we meet Deborah, who was ruling Israel after they had strayed from the Lord and been oppressed by the Canaanites for twenty years under King Jabin and his army commander, Sisera. The people had been crying out for deliverance, and the Lord used Deborah's leadership to fight back against oppression and bring freedom to the people of God.[2]

I've always thought there are hints of frustration in the story of Deborah. I may be reading into the text, but bear with me ...

Take a look at Deborah's victory song in Judges 5. In the previous chapter, we're told that Deborah is leading Israel and that she calls for Barak, from the tribe of Naphtali, to muster an army from his own tribe and from Zebulun. An army from just two of the twelve tribes of Israel? What's going on?

Her song in Judges 5 gives some background to this:

> In the districts of Reuben
> there was much searching of heart.
> Why did you stay among the sheepfolds
> to hear the whistling for the flocks?
> In the districts of Reuben
> there was much searching of heart.
> Gilead stayed beyond the Jordan.
> And Dan, why did he linger by the ships?
> Asher remained on the coast
> and stayed in his coves.[3]

It seems that Deborah had heard a word from the Lord and then sent out messengers and envoys to various tribes to see who was with her. But the answers that came back went something like: no, we're a bit busy; we've got the sheep to look after, the ships to repair ... plus, the enemy's army have chariots fitted with iron ... we know we've been asking the Lord for deliverance, but we're not sure he's really calling us to step up and do anything about it.

The tribes of Reuben, Dan, Asher and those in Gilead all decide to stay where they are; they fail to engage, fail to fight oppression, fail to support their leader.

But two tribes go to war:[4] Naphtali and Zebulun are willing to step up.

So, frustrated at the response of the other tribes – but glad that at least some have responded positively to the vision – Deborah calls Barak, the leader of Naphtali's army.

She says to him, 'The LORD, the God of Israel, commands you: "Go, take with you ten thousand men of Naphtali and Zebulun and lead them up to Mount Tabor. I will lead Sisera, the commander of Jabin's army, with his chariots and his troops to the River Kishon and give him into your hands."'[5]

What is Barak's response? After all the prayer for deliverance, after all the talk about fighting back the oppressor, after just two tribes have responded in faith that God would do what he has said he would do. And after being commissioned by the leader of the country, what does he say?

'If you go with me, I will go; but if you don't go with me, I won't go.'[6]

I've always read a pause between this verse and the next, where Deborah has to pull together all her self-control. The vision is clear. The word of the Lord is that victory is just around the corner. She's raised up a leader, despite some negative responses. And now he doesn't really want to go unless she goes with him.

He's not the confident leader she was hoping he would be. He doesn't have the faith or conviction that she has. In my head, there's verse '8b' where Deborah thinks to herself, *Oh, for goodness' sake. Do I have to do everything?!*

As the one who heard the Lord on this, it's easy for her to have faith about it; the vision is strong in her heart and mind. She's envisioned others, but despite some catching the vision, they don't carry the same level of faith she does.

So, with a deep breath (in my mind's eye, at least) she agrees to go with Barak, but warns him that, because of this, he won't be the one to get the glory for the victory; she will. He seems OK with this compromise and heads off to gather the troops.

And they see the Lord bring the freedom he promised. (And yes, this is the bit of the story where Sisera gets a tent peg through his skull, but that doesn't really help illustrate the point I'm trying to make.)

Frustrations in leadership are hard.

But they can help us *grow*.

Growing Through Frustration

Hebrews 12:7 says to 'Endure hardship as discipline' – when we go through hard times, we can use those times to help us grow. But how?

Read verse 11: 'No discipline seems pleasant at the time, but painful.'

No kidding.

'Later on, however, it produces a harvest of righteousness and peace for those who have been trained by it.'

Here's what it's saying: if we allow ourselves to be trained by the hardship, enduring it as discipline, it produces a harvest (think: joy, abundance, more than you know what to do with) of righteousness (right living, right relationships, right perspective) and peace. Not in that moment, but later on.

Every pearl starts as a piece of grit inside an oyster. An irritant. An imperfection. But look what it turns into. When things don't go as you expected, it might well be painful, it might be frustrating. But that means it's an opportunity to grow.

Holiness: growing to become more like Jesus through our difficulties and frustrations. Remember, holiness equals weight. The more holiness, the heavier the stone. The more we grow like Jesus, the bigger impact we have. Big stones make big ripples.

In that tough season when we were wrecked by *Hannah Montana*, the Lord taught me about using frustration. Most of my prayer life was filled with me telling him what was wrong, why it was wrong and what he should do about it. I vented my frustrations on him.

Don't get me wrong, this is biblical prayer. Read the Psalms – David and other psalmists were often going to the Lord with their frustrations, the things that confused them, the things they wished the Lord would do ('dash their babies on the rocks' … Aren't you glad the Lord is more gracious than we are?![7]).

But one day in prayer I felt the Lord interrupt me and ask if I wanted to use my frustrations for good.[8] I sensed the Lord invite me to use my frustrations to help me grow. The tool I felt he was inviting me to engage with looks like this:

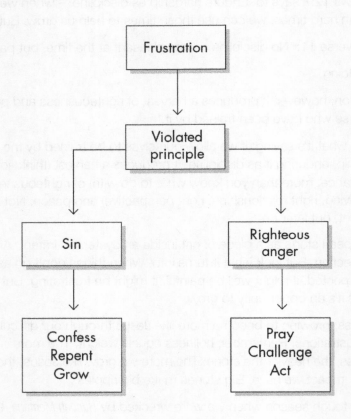

The Holy Spirit pointed out to me that we are usually frustrated because a principle we hold dear has been violated. Say you are stuck in traffic. If you had planned for the traffic, it's annoying to have to wait your turn, nudging slowly towards the intersection, so you can turn through the lights – probably straight into the next line of traffic. But at least you've planned for it, and your expectations for the journey align with reality.

But if you hadn't planned for it, it can be really frustrating. Why? Because of your expectations: the principle you hold dear – punctuality – has been violated, and the traffic is making you late.

Frustrations can help reveal underlying principles – if we are willing to do the work to understand what is going on within us.

Then the Lord invited me to consider these violated principles which have caused frustration in the light of his love and holiness. Is this principle godly, or sinful? Is it my own sin and pride? Or is it righteous anger?

Often it's a mixture of the two, but the Holy Spirit's invitation is to learn more about ourselves in the midst of our frustration, and to be honest about what that frustration shows us of our own brokenness, selfishness or pride.

Three Responses to Sin

The word 'sin' means to miss the mark, or fall short. It can be used in archery when the arrow falls short of the target. Sin isn't a word that's commonly used in today's language, so I've often wondered how I can help someone from a non-church background understand and relate to it.

Instead of talking about sin, I now talk about the places in our lives where we've let God, ourselves and others down. Places where we've missed the mark, or fallen short.

The first response to this is to *confess*: you have to take responsibility and admit – to God and to others – where you were wrong. There's a humility about being willing to take responsibility. Often it's complicated, and it's not entirely our fault, but we need to be humble enough to accept where it is and admit it.

Second, we *repent*: we say sorry, and reflect on how we might have done something differently. To repent means to change – both change our mind and our actions. As we reflect on how we might have done something better, as we ask others for their advice and help, the third response begins.

Third, we *grow*. We recognise that our frustrations were based on principles that came from a place of brokenness. By allowing the Holy

Spirit to identify that brokenness, we allow him access to begin to heal and restore us. It doesn't happen immediately – sometimes it's a life-long lesson – but this is the process of repenting and believing, which Jesus said was the way we step into God's kingdom.[9] And our frustrations can serve us in this way.

However, it may well be, that even when we have made ourselves right with the Lord, there remains some righteous anger. The principle which was violated was a good one, and created valid frustration. Just as there are three responses to sin, which help us grow, there are three responses to righteous anger.

Three Responses to Righteous Anger

The first is to *pray*: asking prayer and listening prayer, in the midst of the frustration. Asking prayer: 'Lord, bring the breakthrough. Lord, help.' Listening prayer: 'Lord, are you asking me to do anything in response to this situation? Lord, what are you trying to show me in this?'

Second, it may be right to *challenge* whatever is causing the righteous anger. For example, when a struggling working family was kicked out of their home, it caused us great frustration – at the landlord and the social housing agency who were responding inadequately. There was little question that this was righteous anger, and so the right thing to do was challenge the relevant authorities. Lizzy and I wrote letters and emails of support. Lizzy got the local councillor and others involved, fighting for what is right at the institutional level. And, on the personal level, doing some loads of washing for them while the situation remained unresolved.

Third, we might need to *do* something to initiate change. Are you frustrated at the presence of modern-day slavery in your city? It may be God stirring you to do something about it. Are you frustrated at the high levels of suicide among young people? It may be God stirring you to do something about it. You get the idea. As Popeye said, 'That's all I can stands, I can't stands no more!' Sometimes frustration burns due to righteous anger, and this is the Lord stirring us to act.

What makes you frustrated? Take a little time to use this tool. What's the underlying principle that has been violated which is now causing you frustration? Now, ask yourself: is the Holy Spirit revealing in me a place of brokenness which needs to be healed? Or, is the Lord revealing some righteous anger which needs me to respond?

As leaders, it's easy to fall into the trap of neglecting our own emotional health, always prioritising those around us before we deal with what's going on inside ourselves. But if we are to lead others well, we need to pay attention to what's going on for us personally, developing our leadership both under the surface and in outward practices; trusting that the Lord recognises our humanity, our weaknesses, our limitations.[10]

Transference and Projection

As disciples and as leaders, we need to acknowledge the impact and influence we can have on others – both positive and negative. Our weaknesses can spill out and adversely impact those around us. We need to own this and do what we can to avoid having a negative impact on others.

However, we also need to recognise that other people's weaknesses can impact us too. One of the most important things we can do is recognise what's going on with both *transference* and *projection*.

Transference is when we treat someone differently by transferring our (often negative) feelings onto them because they remind us of someone else. It's often unhealed hurt from someone in our past. A new person reminds us of them, so we treat them as if they are the person from our past, rather than a new individual. Therapists expect it, and I suggest that we should too. As we lead others and create relationships of trust with them, it's possible (or even likely) that at times those people will transfer onto us.

It's important to build effective boundaries and have a strong sense of self to recognise when others are engaged in transference. But we also need to be able to see when we are transferring onto others. Are we willing to allow the Lord to heal the brokenness within us, so that we can treat everyone as distinct individuals?

Projection can be understood as a form of transference, but instead of transferring bad feelings about someone else onto a person, it's linked more to our own weaknesses. It is 'the unconscious process by which an individual attributes to another the desires, impulses, or ideas that he finds unacceptable in himself'.[11] To explain this on a deeper level: 'Projection provides an illusory and temporary sense of well-being because painful emotions are cast off onto another person.'[12]

You go home in the car after a long hard day at work, frustrated about something you didn't get finished and angry at your boss who undermined you. You get cut up as you're driving home, but when you arrive at the house you say, 'Wow, that guy who cut me up was angry – he had no idea I was there and just pushed right in front of me. I would have crashed if I hadn't slammed on the brakes.'

That's projection. You're hurt and angry because of what happened at work, and so you project onto the other driver – who may have been angry – but it's possible they may just have made an innocent mistake.

Projection happens when we're not willing to own our hurt. It's easier to assume someone else is angry, because if we admit we are angry then we have to deal with it.

It's important that we understand these processes when we are leading and pastoring people who might project onto us – but it's also important that we acknowledge our own brokenness and tendencies.

A leader who is growing in emotional health is someone who is willing to face and work through their weaknesses with trusted others: mentors, prayer partners, a spiritual director, so that they don't remain in the echo chamber of their own making.

I'm so grateful for the New Wine family as it's connected me with peers I can chat with and older, wiser leaders I can learn from. I pray once a month with another local church leader. I also pray together once a month with some of the other church leaders in Manchester. I have a spiritual director I meet three to four times a year. I call wiser, older leaders to ask for their advice and help.

The challenge, you see, is this: we're likely to either take too much responsibility or not enough. I go on retreat with three friends once a year. We spend time together catching up, eating good food, enjoying one another's company; and we spend a couple of hours each, reflecting on the past year and praying for one another. It's oxygen to my soul. Two of us are those who are likely to take too much responsibility – it's all my fault, it's my job to fix everything. Two of us are more inclined to assume it's someone else's problem.

The reality is, it's somewhere in the middle – for both groups. We do have to learn to take responsibility where hurt has been caused, or where someone is upset. But having wise friends and counsel around us can help us to see the truth, and determine the lies.

Do you have people in your life who pray with you, mentor you, support you? Who is helping you grow?

'No' to Good, 'Yes' to Great

As well as growing in emotional health, life is full of external challenges and pressures. Every day we have a choice of how we will use our time. Our life is a precious resource. What we do with our life matters. To grow in maturity is to grow in prioritising our time, giving our attention to the things that truly matter.

Stephen R. Covey, in his fabulous book *The 7 Habits of Highly Effective People*, uses a grid to help determine the difference between important and urgent tasks, and how to prioritise them.[13]

	URGENT	NOT URGENT
IMPORTANT	**Quadrant 1** Urgent and important **DO**	**Quadrant 2** Not urgent but important **PLAN**
NOT IMPORTANT	**Quadrant 3** Urgent but not important **DELEGATE**	**Quadrant 4** Not urgent and not important **ELIMINATE**

You can sit down at the beginning of the day or week and add all your tasks into one of these four boxes.

Important and urgent tasks – those in quadrant one – are crises: responding to a fire, visiting the hospital for someone who was rushed in overnight, hitting a deadline for a funding application, getting the designs sent off for a print run for publicity. These things are important, and because they are time pressured they are also urgent. These are at the top of your priority list. Do them. Now.

The problem is, so often we end up prioritising quadrant three: things that are urgent, but not always important. More often than not, urgent but not important matters mean we are being reactive rather than proactive. A phone call always seems urgent – the ringtone seems to say, 'Answer me now!' – but do you really need to take that call right at this moment? If you're in the middle of finishing something important – writing a report, having a pastoral conversation with someone, spending time in prayer (you get the idea) – you can let the call go to voicemail. If they keep calling, you'll get the impression that it's both urgent and important! Urgent but not important things take up our time, but don't always get us closer to where we are aiming.

Things in quadrant four – those that are not urgent or important – are that new game you just downloaded on your phone. Or some of the emails we receive. Or timewasters – those people who, after you've met with them, don't appear to have listened to a word you said or do anything you've suggested.

Covey's point is that we so often miss out quadrant two: those things that are important but not urgent. Exercise, long-range planning, relationship building, recreation. The things we have to plan for but often never get around to. It's why he calls it a habit – we have to build these things into our lives in a regular way and insist to ourselves and others that it is worth the time investment – because it always is.

Time off is always a tough one for motivated pioneers. But learning to rest means we are not defined by what we do. It helps us avoid being eaten up by the never-ending demands of pioneering and planting. Build in Sabbath time: a day a week to rest and worship, and nothing else.[14]

This requires boundaries which will need to be firm but flexible. Lizzy and I have had to learn this one. Pioneering with your spouse can be the most amazing thing, but also the most challenging. Date nights can turn into staff meetings if you're not careful. We chose to ban talking about work in some rooms in the house. It's harder than it sounds, because we're committed to each other, and both of us are committed to this vision and mission.

What boundaries might you need to develop? When you say to someone in need that you're there for them any time of day or night, is it OK for them to call you at 2 a.m. every night, for a week? When does it become not OK, and how do you let them know?

Boundaries also help us focus on the important and not urgent things. How often are you willing to cancel your time at the gym to meet other people? (I'm guilty of this. I know it's important to exercise, but I find it hard to justify turning down meeting or helping someone so I can work out. I'm getting better at it, but it's still hard.)

How often do you step back and take a look at the bigger picture? How often are you pursuing wise counsel? Do you have a prayer team you can send urgent prayer requests to?

Another important question to ask is this: How do I put my family first? Lizzy and I are really committed to trying to ensure that our kids don't get sacrificed on the altar of mission. We want to prioritise family, and we try to be a family who are on the mission together. This looks like praying together; each member of the family asking God how we are part of this mission he has called us on. Sometimes life just gets crazy busy, so we've tried to build in good rhythms – one of these is to always eat breakfast and dinner together as a family, sitting around the table.

Every morning, we have breakfast and do our 'please and thank yous' – our version of morning prayer – where we ask God for help with something for ourselves or someone else, and express our gratitude to God for something. However we're feeling, there's always something for which we can be thankful.

Then every evening, we try to eat dinner together and do our 'highs and lows': the best bit of the day and the worst bit. It's an opportunity for everyone in the family to speak and be heard, and every so often a profound conversation is kicked off by what's happening in one another's lives. And sometimes, if there's no low, we have a song to celebrate, which includes banging the table and making as much noise as possible. (This is particularly fun when we have guests for dinner!)

Just to be clear: this is hard. It's hard to get up early to have breakfast before the kids set off for school. It's hard to work out when everybody is going to be in for dinner each evening when there are so many other things happening. It takes thought and planning. But before that, it takes prioritising – where we recognise that something is important, and determine to make it happen.

Lizzy and I also try to plan our holidays before anything else gets in the calendar, so that as other things get put in through the year, we have some fixed points when we can be away as a family. It has meant we've had some great family times over the years.

Our kids are teenagers right now, so we don't know the long-term impact of what we're doing. But we have a strong family unit, and we love hanging out together. As the kids get older, they'll become more and more independent, and so we're simply trying to be intentional about establishing healthy rhythms to encourage good relationships within the family, and help them grow in their faith. Our prayer is that it will give them a good foundation in life and faith themselves.

What would a good family rhythm look like for you at your stage of life? How do you remain connected, rested, rooted and supported? If you're single, how can you incorporate meaningful relationships in your life and rhythms, just like Jesus did?

Being intentional is a good way of summing up what it means to grow – not striving, but learning through God's grace that the journey is just as important as the destination. And who we are becoming is just as important as where we are going.

How can you put in good practices and good disciplines to help you grow in this season? Through the good times and the bad, use every opportunity to ask the Lord to make you more like him: more holy, more obedient, more of a blessing to others. Dying to self and living to Christ. Becoming a radical disciple of Jesus. Taking up your cross and following him; putting him first in everything, so that he gets the glory.

Don't try to grow your church without first growing yourself.

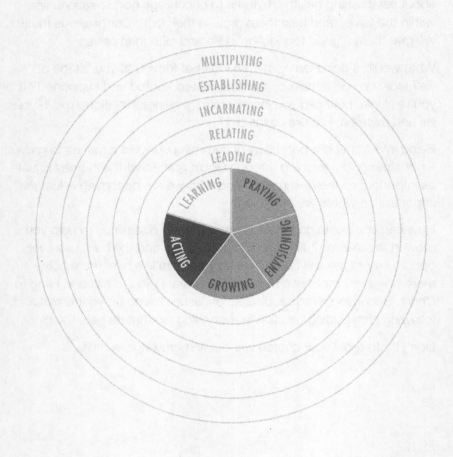

4

Acting

Prayers are powerful. Having a vision is great. Being willing to grow is key. But, eventually, a pioneer has to *do* something.

Start *somewhere*.

Having a vision is not enough. To plant new churches, to pioneer new work, you need to give something a try.

One of my favourite Old Testament characters is Joseph – a dreamer who goes on to do big things. But Joseph had to learn the lesson that to see your dreams fulfilled means *doing* something in response to God's favour, not just waiting for it to fall into your lap.

As a young man, Joseph's major problem was that he expected God to do all the heavy lifting to enable his dreams to come to pass.

Joseph believed the dreams he received, but lorded it over his brothers, presumably expecting them to bow down to him at any minute.[1]

They did the opposite.

There was Joseph, proudly wearing his special coat, which proved he was the most favoured son, walking around as if he owned the place, while the other brothers were just getting on with the work. You get the sense that Joseph was genuinely surprised about his brothers despising him.

He thought his brothers would bow down to him, but instead they grabbed his coat off him and threw him into an empty cistern. Then they sold him into slavery.

On the journey, something changed in Joseph. By the time he got to the slave market, he seemed to have resolved to do things differently. God's favour was still on him, and Joseph started serving and using his gifts in the house of Potiphar.

And it turned out, he could do things pretty well.

Potiphar looked at Joseph and 'saw that the Lord was with him and that the Lord gave him success in everything he did'.[2] So God helped Joseph prosper as he served in the home of his Egyptian master. But here's my point: Joseph got on with stuff, and the Lord gave him success. He acted in response to his circumstances, instead of waiting for things to happen. God was gracious, and Joseph was diligent. Potiphar promoted Joseph to the point where he was running the whole household, and Joseph continued to faithfully serve.

You might argue, Joseph didn't really have a choice – he was a slave who would get punished if he didn't do what he was told. Good point. But he had clearly started to work on his character too; finding himself in a compromising situation with Potiphar's wife, he fled temptation and acted honourably, just as he had been honourable in his work for Potiphar.

Joseph was thrown into jail for something he didn't do. The false accusations must have burned deep inside – he'd tried to do the right thing, but there was a massive power imbalance, and he had no rights, so the conviction stood regardless of its truth, and he ended up in prison.[3]

What would you have done? Joseph had every right to give up. Hated by his brothers, sold into slavery, wrongly accused, thrown into prison. It would have been easy – understandable, even – for Joseph to feel overwhelmed, give up and let prison life mould him into a hopeless character with nothing to live for. As we discovered in the previous chapter, our frustrations and battles can either define us and hold us back, or help us to grow.

But while Joseph was there in the prison, the LORD was with him; he showed him kindness and granted him favour in the eyes of the prison warder. So the warder put Joseph in charge of all those held in the prison, and he was made responsible for all that was done there. The warder paid no attention to anything under Joseph's care, because the LORD was with Joseph and gave him success in whatever he did.[4]

Joseph could have slouched in the corner waiting to die, but instead, when he was given things to do, he got on and did them. He demonstrated diligence, integrity and character, and grew through some really difficult circumstances, all of which turned out to be great training to take on the role of Pharaoh's second-in-command.

This is quite a turnaround from the guy who didn't want to get dirt under his fingernails back in Canaan. Quite a change from the young man who swanned around expecting things to fall into his lap.

Joseph grew into a person who served where he found himself, and in the process, his gifts and skills were developed, so that God's dreams for him could be realised.

Just Do It

It's easier to steer a car when it's moving than when it's stationary. In the same way, if we start moving, while keeping our hearts listening to the Lord, he can steer us in the right direction. However, if we just sit around waiting for his promises to be fulfilled, we might be surprised at how long things take.

Pioneers *do* things. They're activists by nature.

So give something a try.

And if it doesn't work, try to learn from it and leverage the learning into trying something better next time.

Because sometimes things don't work.

In the chapter on envisioning, I described how we ended up running our drop-in centre, Glo Central. It was a great success in many ways, and we even won a gold award for the 'Best Project Advancing the Christian Faith' at the inaugural Christian Funders Forum in 2015.[5]

What I didn't describe in that chapter were some of the other ideas we tried, which failed. When we arrived in Offerton, the local high school was closing down. There was a sense of indignation in the community, and we knew from experience that if you remove a high school from an area, the young people are shipped off to a variety of other schools, resulting in a reduced sense of connection and community.

So I decided we should try to open a Free School.

Free Schools were a new idea at the time; a school run by the local community, formed out of a trust that would be responsible for delivering education in a creative way. Getting the vision was easy: bless both the community and the young people in the local area by establishing a creative arts school, which could help students who struggled in other more formal educational settings to thrive under God's love and great opportunities.

Who wouldn't want to do that?

Well, lots of people, it would seem.

I spent months meeting with various people who might support our cause: those who were most vocal about the school closure on social media, one of the key students, a teacher at the school who I knew from another local church, the local councillor with responsibilities for schools.

I printed out the hundreds of pages of information about Free Schools, how to establish the trust, how to register the school itself. I began to seek funding, so we could try to buy the building from the council.

I did everything I could to get this idea going.

But it completely failed.

It turned out I'd bitten off far more than I could chew. There wasn't the financial support, or the groundswell of the right people gathering around the idea to enable it to happen. I knew I couldn't start a school, open a coffee shop, study for ordination and plant a church at the same time, so I had to choose. It was a real time of growth; a time to lay down a good thing for the sake of the better thing. I'd had vision for the school, I could see it in my mind's eye and I was excited about the possibilities. But I had to let it go.

Pruning is Healthy

Jesus calls this 'pruning'. In John 15 he describes how we cannot be fruitful unless we are getting our nutrients and life from the Vine himself. But part of keeping us healthy and fruitful also involves pruning.

If you're a good gardener,[6] you'll know that not every bud on a rose bush should grow into a stem or flower. Roses produce too much growth for the plant to sustain, and the whole plant can become weak and unhealthy if the gardener allows every bud to grow. Sometimes it's obvious, right from the beginning, that the bud or new stem needs to be pruned. That's like all the ideas flooding through your head: not all of them need to happen *right now*. Some of them may be good for the future; some of them may not be good ideas at all. But we're all limited, and it's a paradox that our growth and maturity sometimes are demonstrated in *not* doing something, in pruning back the plant.

Lizzy is amazing at coming up with great ideas. Before we've even started breakfast, she has usually had a couple of ideas of things we could do. But if we followed through on every idea she had we'd be exhausted, and we would deliver poorly on all of them. Why? Because we're limited. We're human.

So try things, and don't worry too much about whether or not they fail. Be concerned for the people involved, of course – love and pastor them through something not working the way you expected or hoped – but put your hope in the Lord, not your project. Keep your eyes on him, not your success. God can take a convicted criminal and turn him into the second most important official in the most powerful empire the world had ever seen.

Pioneering and planting has very close links to being an entrepreneur. In many ways, it demands the same skills, the same way of thinking, the same tenacity. I once heard a stat that most successful entrepreneurs in the US have gone bankrupt eight times. I can't find anything to back this up, but the point is clear: to do something successful, you have to be prepared to try, and fail, and try again. Keep going.

Michael Jordan, 'the greatest basketball player of all time', is quoted as saying this about failure:

> I've missed more than 9,000 shots in my career. I've lost almost 300 games. Twenty-six times I've been trusted to take the game-winning shot and missed. I've failed over and over and over again in my life. And that is why I succeed.[7]

My key point here is this: we can only discern where God is at work when we give things a try. Pioneers try. Pioneers do. Pioneers go. Sometimes the ideas succeed, and sometimes they fail – but failed plans don't make you a failure. If something fails, reflect, learn, develop: if at first you don't succeed, try, try and try again.

How does the idea of pruning make you feel? Have you ever had to bring things to an end because they didn't work out the way you'd hoped? What have you started that succeeded? Are there any principles you can learn from what you did, and how you did it, to help you the next time you start something new?

There is, of course, a balance between getting on with things, and waiting for God to do something. Prayer always goes alongside acting. Keep asking the Lord: is this the right thing? Is this the right time? Is this the right path?

Praying for discernment is key, but we pray as we journey, asking God to direct our steps.

People of Peace

When Jesus sent his followers off on mission, he prepared them for both success and failure. Reading through Luke 10 gives us some great insight into the instructions he gave them, and we can learn a lot from listening in.

First, the disciples were commissioned by Jesus. They were sent out, as we are, under his authority. They were to visit the towns where Jesus was planning to go and announce that he was on his way. And then Jesus reminded them of the vision: 'The harvest is plentiful, but the workers are few.'[8] The harvest is plentiful – there are loads of people out there just waiting to hear the good news of God's kingdom revealed in Jesus. Look at all that is possible!

Then, in the same verse, Jesus calls the disciples to pray: 'Ask the Lord of the harvest, therefore, to send out workers into his harvest field.' As is so often with the Lord, when we start to pray, we get caught up in his heart and desire and begin to get a vision of what part we might play in furthering God's kingdom. The disciples are praying for workers – and they are the ones about to do the work. Often, we are the solution to our prayers. Vision and prayer are great places to start as we begin to step into using the authority of Jesus to share God's love and power.

And then Jesus gives his disciples a warning: 'I am sending you out like lambs among wolves.'[9]

Wait, *what?*

Wolves eat lambs for breakfast. Literally. They tear them apart. They are ruthless. They salivate when they see a lamb come near.

Sounds a bit like the words Jesus used in Luke 9 to help the disciples realise what it would take for him to triumph over evil: 'Whoever wants to be my disciple must deny themselves and take up their cross daily and follow me.'[10]

It's not always going to be easy, stepping out in faith on mission. But it wasn't easy for Jesus either, and that should be of some comfort as we seek to invest in eternal, rather than worldly things.

After this caution and realistic preparation, Jesus then tells the disciples to look out for the 'person of peace' – the one who welcomes them, listens to them and helps them. These are the people who would be interested in the conversations about Jesus, and offer the disciples hospitality.

We don't live in first-century Israel, so our customs around hospitality are different. So how does this transpose to our day and age?

One morning, after having recently moved house, Lizzy and I woke up and found our neighbour by our car with a dustpan and brush. It turned out that someone had broken in through the window overnight, and our neighbour was clearing up the glass on the road and inside the car. We were so grateful for this and got into conversation with her. She had been wondering what we did, as so many people came and went from our home; her guess was that we were either swingers or drug dealers! We explained we were Christians, and she was thrilled – she had been asking God to send someone to help her understand more about faith. She joined our small group and started following Jesus.

She welcomed us, listened to us and helped us. A person of peace.

Who are your people of peace? Are there people around you who, although they may not yet be Christians, welcome you, listen to you and help you? When you give something a go, try not to do it alone – see if the activity itself can create the opportunity to connect with people of peace. So, do things *with* people, not *for* people.

Jesus was really clear that there would also be those who would not welcome, listen and help. So what should we do then? What's a twenty-first-century version of taking off your shoes, wiping the dust off your feet as a warning and letting people know the kingdom of God is coming, whether they like it or not?[11] My understanding of this is that we entrust the individual to Jesus, and move on. We can't force anything on anyone. We have no right to tell people what to believe. All we can be responsible for is our own actions, what we do and who we tell about Jesus. How others respond is up to them.

Jesus sums it up in verse 16: 'Whoever listens to you listens to me; whoever rejects you rejects me; but whoever rejects me rejects him who sent me.' Learning to forgive, allowing people to disagree with you, loving your enemies and praying for those who persecute you. These things help us *grow*. It turns out *acting* is another way of becoming more mature, more holy, if we allow ourselves to be trained by it.

Rejection and Accusation

Nobody likes being rejected. We recently launched an Alpha course, and as a church we have been praying for three people every day for three weeks. I was pumped for the people I was praying for and had a conversation with one of them just a few days after I started to pray. He told me how tough he was finding things and that he was looking for answers and fulfilment. He had previously said he was interested in doing Alpha, so I encouraged him to try it out, and he seemed keen. Then, as I followed up before the launch party, he texted me saying *no, thanks*, it wasn't his thing.

I was gutted.

And it was hard to hear. Was I too pushy? Did I ask the wrong way? Am I not very good at sharing my faith? Does he not like me? What will I say next time I see him? Am I a bad Christian? On top of all that, the other two people I was praying for also turned down the invitation.

Ugh. I'm no good at this. What kind of a church planter am I?

Of course, the accuser – Satan – loves all this.[12] He throws all his weight behind these kinds of thoughts (plus, he loves it when we do his job for him, speaking unhealthy thoughts about ourselves that don't line up with God's view of us). 'What are people going to think of you? You're no good. You might as well give up. God thinks you're a failure. People are laughing at you behind your back.'

Wait a second. I'm meant to 'take captive every thought to make it obedient to Christ'.[13] I'm loved by the Father, saved by grace, and the Holy Spirit dwells in me. I've seen his power at work through me. All that happened was that three people I invited to Alpha said *no, thanks*.

So instead of beating myself up and listening to my feelings of rejection, I've entrusted those three people to Jesus. I'll keep praying for them. I'll keep loving them. But I won't take responsibility for their decision about Jesus – that's between him and them. I'll do my best to be kind and represent the King well, but if they choose not to follow him, I must respect that choice and honour them.

The same is true of the Free School idea. I could have got angry at the people who didn't want to support it. I could have tried harder and worked more hours. The accuser was certainly hard at work on me – 'Why can't you see vision come to reality? What kind of leader are you? What will all the people think after you told them this was a great idea?'

Well, it was a great idea. But I trust that because there weren't very many people of peace to help make it a reality, it wasn't a *God* idea. It was just me trying to be like Joseph – working out what I could do in the circumstances where I found myself. Joseph discovered it's more important to look for and respond to God's favour, to get on and serve diligently where you find yourself, than be caught up in your dreams and ideas. Focus on loving and serving others where you are, and look for the people of peace who will help you by supporting the kingdom activity.

Are you so easily distracted by the big dreams and ideas that you don't get round to loving and serving others? What can you do now, what can you try now, which would mean you're not just dreaming but doing? So that your faith is not just ideas, but action?

Jesus was clear: some people will listen, and others will reject. It was true for him, so it will be true for us too. Some things will work great, and others will fail, but we keep doing what we can. Just like Joseph, doing our best in the place we find ourselves, and trusting that God can and will work it for our good.

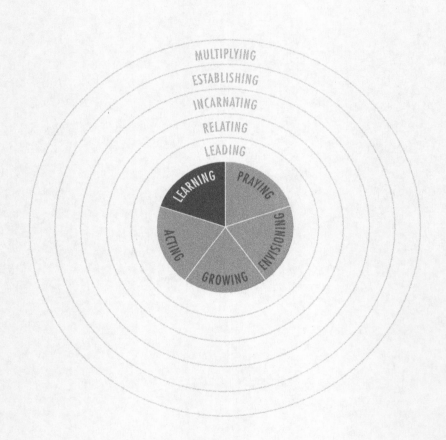

5

Learning

You may have picked up already that these five characteristics are very much interlinked. You can't get vision without prayer; you can't grow without doing something new; you can't work out what to do without vision ...

This final characteristic is closely tied to the other four, but distinct in its own way. If growing is about becoming more whole as a person, learning is about developing the right gifts and skills, along with understanding our context and the people we are seeking to reach.

To follow Jesus is to be his disciple. And, as perhaps you know, the word disciple means 'learner', or 'student'.

The disciples called Jesus 'Rabbi', which means teacher.

Teacher and learners.

We never stop being disciples of Jesus; we never graduate beyond being learners. We might become skilled at something, but pride must be avoided at all costs, otherwise we might start doing things without looking to the Master first.

In fact, we can end up doing Sunday church without looking to the Master. Church-like services are really easy to do without God. There's an organisation called Sunday Assembly, which does exactly that – an atheist congregation going through the motions of church, literally without God.[1] It proves that simply the act of gathering together, singing some songs, listening to someone share something, and taking time to ponder and reflect, creates a meaningful environment for people.

But how awful would it be to realise that our church services are more like a Sunday Assembly – well planned, interesting, engaging, but completely devoid of God's presence and power?

That's why we need the Holy Spirit, and we need to create room for him when we gather, to do what only he can do. It's one of the things I love most about New Wine – a family of churches committed to making space for the Holy Spirit to work in the midst of all our plans and good ideas. To take a moment, whenever we gather, to pray 'Come, Holy Spirit', and then wait to see what he does. To expect the Holy Spirit to be involved in our daily lives, to speak to us, lead us, guide us, prompt us to speak to someone, intervene through us in someone's life with a miracle that draws them to Jesus.

The Holy Spirit helps us learn about God's perspective, God's will. Jesus said, 'when he, the Spirit of truth, comes, he will guide you into all the truth. He will not speak on his own; he will speak only what he hears, and he will tell you what is yet to come.'[2]

It's the gifts of the Spirit that make the church distinct, helping it function and be formed into the body of Christ. And Scripture makes it clear: we need each other. 'Now to each one the manifestation of the Spirit is given for the common good.'[3] By allowing the Holy Spirit to work through us, we can grow and mature as the full expression of the church:

> Christ himself gave the apostles, the prophets, the evangelists, the pastors and teachers, to equip his people for works of service, so that the body of Christ may be built up until we all reach unity in the faith and in the knowledge of the Son of God and become mature, attaining to the whole measure of the fullness of Christ.[4]

The Holy Spirit guides us to learn and grow, to become mature together. To seek God's will and be learners of him.

Learning How We Learn

So *how* do we learn? To answer this question, it's worth asking how the disciples of Jesus learned.

By being with Jesus.

When we see Jesus in others, when we read the Scriptures and learn about how Jesus lived, when we allow the Holy Spirit access to our lives to guide us into all truth, we are learning as disciples of Jesus.

The Twelve watched and listened to Jesus, in private sessions and in public. He allowed them access to his life, and through this process they learned what it meant to function in the way he did. After watching, they gave it a go themselves.

In Luke's telling of the story, we can see that Jesus took his disciples through the four steps of training:

I do, you watch.
I do, you help.
You do, I help.
You do, I watch.

I Do, You Watch

Let's look at Luke 4:31–44.

Jesus had started his ministry after his baptism, and had gone to the town of Capernaum. Simon lived in Capernaum, and may have heard about Jesus from friends in other towns close to where Jesus had already been. We can confidently assume that Simon was at the synagogue on the day Jesus preached there. He was likely among the crowd that was 'amazed at his teaching, because his words had authority'.[5]

It was also the day that Jesus delivered someone from an unhealthy spirit, right there in front of everyone, without any drama or special prayers; simply with a command, with authority and with love.

Simon invited Jesus back to his place. And there, in Simon's own house, Jesus healed his mother-in-law from a high fever. It seemed word spread – that evening, people brought their sick friends and relatives for Jesus to heal, and he delivered people from unhealthy spirits.

Wow!

Simon may have then heard Jesus leave the house very early the next morning, heading off to pray. (Or, at least, they found his bed empty when they came to offer him breakfast.) Simon watched Jesus heal and deliver people, teach with authority, prioritise prayer and remain obedient to God's call, all in those twenty-four hours.

To learn, we have to see something modelled.

Lizzy has taught me loads about evangelism. I'm naturally a shy person, and when I tried to share my faith in Jesus as a younger person it was often clunky. I mean, *very* clunky. The first person I invited to follow Jesus was someone at school. I think I did an OK job of explaining why I thought Jesus was worth following, but then I basically bullied him into praying a prayer to accept Jesus – I wouldn't let him go back to class until he had prayed it! Effective, but not a great long-term strategy.

Lizzy, on the other hand, is a born evangelist. She can't stop herself from telling other people about something good. She finds a great new TV series – everyone needs to know. We discover an amazing campsite – Lizzy tells every person she can about it.

And when it comes to telling people about Jesus, she is so natural. There's no clunkiness about it at all. She just brings up her faith in conversation, tells people what an impact it's made in her life, offers to pray for them and – boom!

I marvelled while I watched it happen. And then I tried it myself. Admittedly it was pretty forced the first few times I gave it a go; I was consciously incompetent, and I got better only as I practised and listened to Lizzy's feedback and coaching – which is the next stage of learning.

Who can you learn from, just by watching them? Who looks more like Jesus than you do in a certain area? Can you ask them to show you how they do it, how they learned? Can they begin to teach you so you become more like them, and so you become more like Jesus?

I Do, You Help

Take a look at Luke 5:1–11.

A few days, weeks or months after leaving, Jesus went back to Capernaum. Instead of preaching in the synagogue, he wanted to use Simon's boat to speak to the people who had gathered there to listen. So there was Simon, literally trapped in his own boat, listening to Jesus. All well and good.

But then, after he finished teaching, Jesus suggested they go fishing. The fishermen, who had just finished their night shift, knew from good experience that you don't go out fishing in the daytime. Add to that, they'd had a terrible night, catching nothing.

Simon remembered the authority with which Jesus taught, and so responded by saying, 'because you say so, I will let down the nets'.[6]

They caught so many fish that their nets started to break.

(I'd love to see Jesus' face at this moment, cracking with a smile of joy, watching Simon and his friends try to deal with all the fish, and then deal with their boats beginning to sink because of how many they had caught.)

Jesus did it, but he allowed Simon to get involved.

We learn by being invited to join in with someone. I learned how to plug in microphones and make them work by following around the guy at church who ran the PA system, and he let me have a go. He showed me what went where and how to work out why things might not be working. He was overseeing it, making sure it was all going to plan, while I helped. I wasn't responsible, but eventually I was able to take responsibility because he had allowed me to learn by helping him.

If you're not great at something, who can help you get better? Not just by watching them, but by helping them do what they do. So that it's not just theory, but practice.

You Do, I Help

Now we move to Luke 6–9.

So Simon had started to follow Jesus and had seen more healings, spent more time wondering where Jesus had got to (as he often went away to pray on his own), as well as hearing him teach and get into arguments with both the Pharisees and the teachers of the law. On top of all that, he watched Jesus go to a party with a bunch of tax collectors, and defend snacking on the Sabbath.

New things for a fisherman. Constantly learning, and being pushed out of his comfort zone.

Then one morning, after Jesus returned from wherever he'd spent the night – a mountainside somewhere – he called his disciples to him. He said he'd been praying through the night, and then 'chose twelve of them, whom he also designated apostles'.[7]

Apostle means 'sent one'. It can also be translated 'missionary'. These were the select few who were not only called to follow Jesus, but given extra responsibility, to share in the mission and ministry of Jesus. Notice, however, what happened next. They may have been designated as missionaries, but the first thing Jesus did with them was teach them the Sermon on the Mount.

Stan Lee was right: with great power comes great responsibility.[8]

After this teaching they went back to Capernaum and continued travelling to different towns around the region, learning and helping out a bit too. Then comes chapter 9. Jesus released the twelve apostles to have a go at doing what he'd been doing: 'he sent them out to proclaim the kingdom of God and to heal those who were ill'.[9]

Once they returned, they reported back everything they had done, and

Jesus invited them to go away with him – a planned holiday (though they were followed, so it didn't turn out quite as planned). Then the Twelve, perhaps having grown in confidence in sharing the mission with Jesus, suggested that Jesus dismiss the crowds – they're hungry, after all, and a long way from anywhere.

'You give them something to eat.'[10]

Say what, now?

There were about five thousand men there (perhaps some had brought their families too). How in the world were they going to do that? Jesus took the only food they were able to find – five loaves of bread and two fishes – and asked the disciples to sit the people down in groups. He blessed the food, gave it to the Twelve, and told them to distribute it.

Where have you learned to take responsibility in your faith journey from someone who has let you give things a try, while watching over you? Maybe learning to pray for others, perhaps in speaking out prophetically, or in caring for the sick or dying?

I remember the first time I led worship at a New Wine summer conference. Initially, I had been allowed to stand at the back of the stage and play my guitar (which I don't think was plugged in!). I watched the worship leader, the band and the people in the Showering Pavilion where we met for worship. And then, one session, it was my turn to lead. My guitar was plugged in, and this time I was at the front of the stage, not the back. The main worship leader was still there too, just in case anything went wrong. I was doing, he was helping.

Back to the feeding of the five thousand. Jesus delegated responsibility to the Twelve, not by dumping them in it but by being present to assist when needed, to help them reflect on what was going on, and drawing them in ever closer. Straight after, they had the conversation during which Peter declared that Jesus is the Messiah. But it was private, intimate sharing: 'Jesus strictly warned them not to tell this to anyone.'[11]

As we grow in responsibility, the invitation is to grow in intimacy with the Lord at the same time. We're not just delegated tasks by God but invited into friendship with him, and to function as his friends.[12]

We learn about God, about ourselves, about others, about our contexts, bit by bit – by taking responsibility and having someone around who can help us reflect, grow and learn. We all need places where we are supported and challenged.

When we're going through challenging times, it's good to receive support from others. Without being challenged, we're unlikely to learn anything new. Contexts where there is support without challenge create a lazy, cosy atmosphere where people are not fulfilling their potential. But overdoing challenge, without support, creates burnout and bitter people.

Jesus offers both. When the disciples were afraid of the Pharisees, Jesus was able to say, 'Do not be afraid, little flock, for your Father has been pleased to give you the kingdom.'[13] But he also didn't hold back in bringing the challenge to Peter of 'Get behind me, Satan!'[14]

Who supports and challenges you? Who do you turn to for wise counsel and advice? What things do you think you still need to learn? Who has already walked the path you're taking, and can help you learn?

You Do, I Watch

Finally, let's consider Acts 1–2.

The final step of learning is to be entrusted with something. After Jesus had completed his ministry, he passed it on to his disciples – *it's over to you now, guys.*

But he didn't leave us alone to have to get through without him: 'you will receive power when the Holy Spirit comes on you; and you will be my witnesses in Jerusalem, and in all Judea and Samaria, and to the ends of the earth'.[15]

Or, as Matthew writes it, 'surely I am with you always, to the very end of the age'.[16]

You might say, the Holy Coach.

I love tennis. As a teenager I went through a season when I would play it most days. I'm not very good, and I had a coach who helped me improve (though they didn't have great raw material to work with). Once I won a competition to a day in London where we could develop our serve, with none other than Goran Ivanišević – who at the time had the most powerful serve in the game.

At the end of the day we were given the opportunity to face his serve. We all stood around the court as the David vs Goliath interactions began. It was so exciting to be up close to see the raw power with which he served. It was also pretty clear to us that, even after a day of coaching, we weren't ready to face this guy. (Honestly, I was pretty thankful I never got chosen to stand on the receiving end!)

After a pretty amazing career in world tennis (winning twenty-two career titles and Wimbledon itself), Ivanišević is now coaching others. And he doesn't coach just anyone. At the time of writing, he coaches Novak Djokovic, one of the best tennis players in the world.

Even the best players in the world still need a coach. They don't get to a point where they think, *Oh, I'm good enough now; I've learned all I need to learn; I'm pretty good at what I do; I don't need a coach.*

No, they keep learning.

You'd think that someone with Djokovic's level of skill, fitness and ability could afford to take it a little easy. But no, to stay at the top of his game he recruits the best people he can find to help him learn more.

Who are the best people you can continue to learn from? Who has led in a way you respect and would like to model? Where in your life and ministry would you still like to improve?

Learning from Mistakes

We never stop being disciples of Jesus, but we get to choose how much we learn, how much access he has to our lives, how willing we are to reflect and grow. Theologians call this 'reflective practice' – continuing to reflect on what's going on, what we're doing, how it's going, what we could learn. It's how our learning community did our pioneering and planting research that led to the book you are holding in your hands.

I've tried to make a routine out of reflective practice, to ensure I keep learning, rather than just presuming or hoping it might happen. Every six months or so we take our team away from the normal pattern of work to reflect, to pray, to dream and to plan.

What's going well? Where could we improve? What's frustrating us? Why? Is there anything we can do about it?

How do you build in time to reflect and learn?

Learning means being aware that change can happen. Sometimes change is out of our control: a volunteer team leader steps down; a grant runs out; illness strikes a key team member. But then other times we might conclude that change needs to happen, and we're the ones to do something about it.

Stopping things can be hard, and the decision needs to be taken after some thought and wise counsel – nobody, after all, likes a leader who keeps changing their mind. (Being flexible is not the same as being indecisive.) Similarly, nobody likes being around a leader who refuses to change their plans despite circumstances working out rather differently than expected.

We launched two groups within the first eighteen months of planting Saint Philips: a toddler group, and an after-school kids club. ChapelTots, our toddler group, started straight after the school run so parents could drop off their kids at school and come along for a coffee. It was an early start for the team to set up, and pretty depressing when only a few parents came with their little ones. Lizzy, who was running it, kept it going – working hard to let parents at the school gates know about it, getting up early with the team to set it all up, only to be disappointed again at how few would come.

So it was time to reflect: what's going on? We've done our best. What can we learn? What can we do better? Lizzy talked with parents and decided to move the group to start an hour later, to give parents and carers time to get home from the school run, get things ready while the toddlers had a nap, and bring them out again for the group. Suddenly it began to grow, word spread and ChapelTots began to be the blessing we always wanted it to be.

The work with kids at our church is top class, and people join and stay with us because of it. We launched our after-school kids club, KidsLife for children aged 7–11, with great vision and excitement. It was ninety minutes of high energy, run by an amazing team who gave it their all. But the kids just didn't come. We did all that we could, but it didn't grow. We tried to put into action the things we had learned from ChapelTots. But, sadly, it didn't see an increase in numbers, and we finally had to conclude that the energy the team were putting into it might be better used elsewhere. It was a hard day when we shared the decision. But it was the right decision.

Lizzy and I have held on to two key concepts to help us learn from our mistakes. First, John Wimber's concept of 'fly or die' – a bit like Gamaliel in the Sanhedrin. He was the guy who spoke up when Peter and John stood accused of healing the lame man at the temple in the name of Jesus. Gamaliel said to the court, 'if their purpose or activity is of human origin, it will fail. But if it is from God, you will not be able to stop these men; you will only find yourselves fighting against God.'[17]

Fly or die: if this grows, God's blessing it. If not, it will die out on its own. We want the people within our church to feel championed and supported, so if someone comes to us with an idea, more often than not we'll encourage them to give it a go. If it flies, great. If it dies, not much has been lost – as long as those invested in it are asking the question, what can we learn?

This is why the second concept we've stolen is Neil Cole's great idea about having a 'shelf of shame' – celebrating those things you tried that just didn't work.[18] It's an idea that's gained traction in large companies like Google, Procter & Gamble and others too.[19] We've learned to celebrate the trying more than the success. We honour those who gave something a go. We cheer on the leaders who stepped out in faith. We ask, what can we learn?

If this is the case, then failure isn't when something didn't succeed.

Failure is not trying.

Keep Learning

Reflecting and learning isn't just about what you're up to – it's also about where you find yourself. You can learn about your context through studying the history of the local area, prayer walking and asking for prophetic discernment, getting to know the various metrics the local councils use to help inform their decisions, researching the particular demographic you are trying to reach in a new context. Who has been successful at doing something similar? What can you learn from them? There is always more to learn, and dozens of ways to do so.

How can you be diligent in learning as much as you can about your focus of mission, whether it's geographic or demographic? Is there someone already doing a similar thing somewhere that you can learn from?

The pioneer and planter needs similar skills to an entrepreneur, and our research from our learning community suggested that learning these basic leadership tools and skills can be a real benefit.

Learn how people work, and how teams work. Using tools like the Myers-Briggs personality type, or the Enneagram, or DiSC, can help us learn about ourselves and others, and how we respond to different circumstances.

We've used the 5 Love Languages test with our teams, so that we can try to better understand how they give and receive love.[20] Lizzy's love language is words of affirmation. She encourages people with words, and loves it when people speak to her with words that affirm who she is and what she's doing. So she kept encouraging a particular person on our team, who was finding things tough, but it was making no difference. This person continued to struggle, regardless of how many times Lizzy would encourage her, text her, write her a note … until we realised that words of affirmation weren't her love language. We'd done the test with the team previously, so looked up the results: quality time.

All the words had impacted her like water off a duck's back. So Lizzy invited her out for a coffee. The difference was almost immediate. To quote the book, her 'love tank' was being filled, and quality time became a key part of leading and loving her well.[21]

It's said that leaders are readers. That's because they keep on learning. What can you put in place to ensure you keep learning? Read books, go on courses, become the best you can be at what you do. Learning how to line manage and supervise a team is key to helping bring the best out of people. Learn how to fundraise, both from the people you are leading, and the grant-making bodies who might support you. Learn how to budget and plan effectively, and learn to be flexible when your plans don't come about.

I'm not saying I've got this all down. But I'm learning.

In God's kingdom, where Jesus is King and Teacher, we never graduate from being learners – there's always something new to learn.

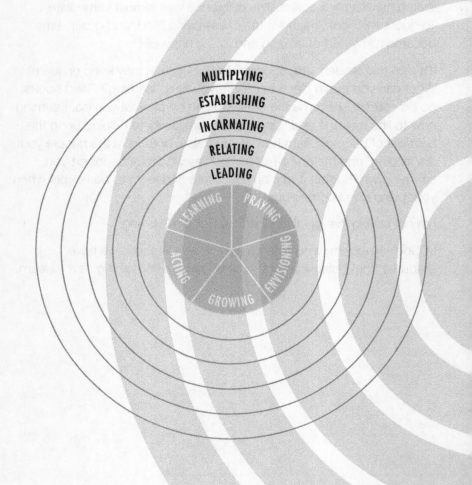

MULTIPLYING

ESTABLISHING

INCARNATING

RELATING

LEADING

LEARNING PRAYING

ACTING ENVISIONING

GROWING

SECTION **TWO**

RIPPLES

It starts with you.

Think of everything we've talked about so far: it's about honing what God has given you so it ripples out of you.

That's why this book started with the five characteristics. It starts with you, building them into your own life, so you can then encourage those characteristics in others.

I recently taught at the final evening of our 'Introduction to Leadership' course at church. I was explaining the principle of leadership as influence — that, as we invest in others, we share with them what God has given us. In turn, those people then influence others for good, and the influence continues to grow. (More of that in the next chapter.) I shared how we planted with twenty-three people, nine of whom were children, and how the work of our church was limited by the size of the team. It would have been impossible for those twenty-three people alone to pull off the ministries and projects that had developed over the previous three years.

It's only because others caught the vision and sensed God's call on their lives to join in – either following Jesus for the first time, or as they move to a new city and look for a new church – that we have been able to do all we're currently doing.

One of our young adults stuck her hand up and said: 'It's a bit like a stone you throw in the water. It makes a plop, which is like a leader having a vision and beginning to make an impact. Then as others gather around the vision and the team, it's like a ripple going out. Then that impacts others, so more join in, which is like the next ripple going out ...'

Yep.

I laughed and told her she'd beautifully summarised the entirety of this book.

That's exactly the dream God has for you – to be fruitful, to bear fruit, fruit that will last.[1] And that's what the ripples are all about.

As we looked at the principles identified by the pioneers and planters who gathered together at our learning communities, it was clear that different people were at different places on the journey of pioneering. This meant that different principles were at work, which affected where their energy was focused.

This is an important concept for us to understand: different stages of growth and multiplication demand different things from us.

Mapping the Way

These five steps will, I hope, help to function as a map for you as you step out in faith. I hope you will use it as a diagnostic tool, to ask: which stage are we in right now? And what does that stage demand of me, of us? I also hope it will help you plan and prepare well for the next stage.

The ripples are how God multiplies things out from us into others, and impacts the world.

That's why the five characteristics are so important: the stone that gets thrown in has an impact on what ripples out.

We considered in the chapter on praying the great, but terrifying question: if someone modelled their prayer life on yours, what would it look like?

Take any number of other metrics from the New Testament.

If someone modelled their thought life on how you deal with lust?

Or based their consumption of alcohol on your behaviour?

How they talk about other people behind their back?

Hospitality?

Dealing with money?

Relationship with spouse, if married?

Self-control?

These are the kinds of things Paul writes about to Timothy, as he describes the qualities of a leader.[2]

It's a reminder to us – before we look at the steps a pioneer takes to go from vision to multiplication – that holiness, obedience and humility are more important than knowing the right steps to take.

Just as we don't want to end up with a Sunday Assembly – church without God – I don't want to pretend that you can pioneer or plant without God. You can, if you'd like. But I hope the characteristics we looked at function as a constant reminder to us that in the midst of all the activity we're about to discuss, our praying, envisioning, growing, acting and learning continue as vital aspects of what we're doing.

Our pioneering and planting research suggests there are five steps to go from vision to multiplication. I can't tell you how long each stage will take, as different contexts demand different things.

When we planted Glo Church in Offerton, Stockport, we took a year with our team before we did anything public. We worshipped together every Sunday afternoon, and met together to grow in our discipleship and to pray as a team every Thursday evening. For a whole year.

In Salford, we had five days.

We had secured funding to employ a team, so we were able to recruit some staff to join us, and we had run a couple of vision nights, but our launch was on the Tuesday evening when we had two hundred well-wishers, including friends and family from all over. The following Sunday morning we kicked off with our first service. It all felt very, very different to our experience in Stockport.

So there's no to-do list, or get-this-done-by-then instructions. It's more like the map of the London Underground: a stylised version of the journey you're likely to take as you pioneer or plant.

Five Steps

The journey starts with *leading* yourself, and then others. As Dwight D. Eisenhower, five-star General through World War II and US president from 1953–1961, famously said, 'The supreme quality for leadership is unquestionably: integrity.' What does it mean to lead with integrity, and serve others by leading them well?

Then it's about *relating* to others: recruiting and building a team, dealing with relational difficulties, and keeping on sharing the vision with those you lead, those you partner with, and those to whom you are responsible.

Once the vision and values have been taught and caught, the work becomes about the context where you are serving, *incarnating* the good news of Jesus to those God is calling you to serve. What does it look like to bring the gospel in the flesh to a group of people – incarnating the love of God as individuals, and as a community?

As with any community, structures, rhythms and routines are needed to sustain the common life – the work of *establishing*, so that the church might grow strong and effective. As you share the good news of Jesus and people are joining in with the vision and coming to faith, how does the fledgling community know when it meets or what its common touch points are? Without them, it's not truly community.

Then it's about *multiplying*, expanding that influence into other people. How can we effectively raise others up to share leadership responsibility and send out leaders to plant and pioneer new work elsewhere?

These are the ripples, the five steps to go from vision to multiplication. And note, you don't stop doing one to start the next; they all build on each other. You can't establish what you don't have, so leading, relating and incarnating need to continue as you do the work of establishing. You get the idea.

I would argue that just as the impact of the stone is based on holiness and obedience, the ripples are affected by our willingness to serve.

Jesus came not to be served, but to serve.[3]

Seeing Others Flourish

Our desire in planting churches or pioneering new work for the Lord is to see others flourish. In their book, *For the Life of the World*, Miroslav Volf and Matthew Croasmun argue that this is the role of academic theology. I would argue that it is also the role of church planting and pioneering new forms of church. They write,

> The purpose of theology [is] to discern, articulate, and commend visions of and paths to flourishing life in light of the self-revelation of God in the life, death, resurrection, exaltation, and coming in glory of Jesus Christ, with this entire story, its lows and its highs, bearing witness to a truly flourishing life.[4]

Theology is the theory. Church is the practice.

It's through the lives and community of those who follow Jesus that this flourishing life is worked out. Imagine church being a place where a vision for flourishing life is discerned, articulated and lived out.

That's not what most people expect from church.

Most people expect a cold, largely empty building, which is generally irrelevant to most of their lives. They're not expecting to find people whose lives are flourishing – and a place where they too might flourish.

To bring the best out of people is to serve them, to love them. It's easy to get side-tracked by structures and plans and vision and admin, but what keeps us on the straight and narrow, what causes the ripples to have the greatest effect, is loving and serving others.

So the filter we see things through, the metric we use to measure, is service. As we are leading, relating, incarnating, establishing and multiplying, the key question to ask on the journey is this: are we serving others as we do this?

Stepping into leadership is about serving other people, not proving we're a good leader or someone worth following.

When we relate to other people and workers within other institutions, are we seeking to serve them, or get what we can from them?

As we incarnate the gospel in our local context, are we doing it to serve the people, or set up a great project we've always dreamed of running?

Do the systems, rhythms and routines you set up for the growing community serve you, or those within it? How can we establish things to help our people flourish?

These next five chapters are about us picking up our towels, wrapping them around our waist, getting down on our knees and washing feet. To serve and not be served.

Just like Jesus.

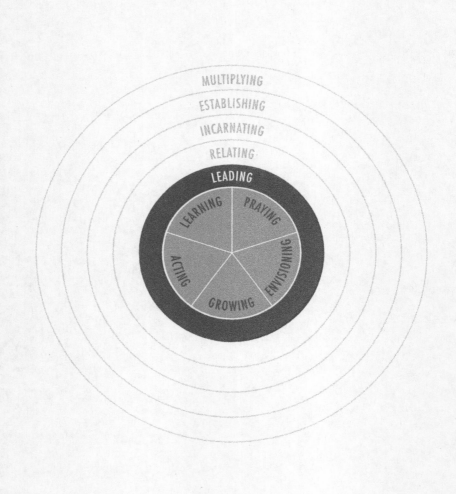

MULTIPLYING

ESTABLISHING

INCARNATING

RELATING

LEADING

LEARNING

PRAYING

ACTING

ENVISIONING

GROWING

6

Leading

What's in you will ripple out of you.

Just as the DNA of a child is set by its parents, so the DNA of a church plant or new project is set by those who plant it. Both nature and nurture are at work in church planting.

The *nature* of the church plant is connected to the geographic or demographic context into which you're planting; the natural gifting that you as a leader and the team bring to the table; and other factors beyond your control.

And *nurture* is about *leading*; seeing what God has given you ripple out into others.

John Maxwell, *The New York Times* bestselling author and 'the most popular leadership and management expert in the world',[1] writes that 'leadership is influence – nothing more, nothing less'.[2]

The question is, how will you influence people?

Think back to when you were in school. I bet you can remember the person who didn't care about breaking the rules, smoking behind the bike sheds, or bunking off lessons and getting others to do it with them.

These people were influencing others – in getting up to no good.

One of the guys in our church is a policeman. He says that those at the top of organised crime are excellent leaders and highly influential. Sadly, they use this to bring harm to others.

If we are going to bring good to others, and influence their lives positively, it demands that we know ourselves – that we're honest about who we are, our weaknesses, brokenness and frailties. We seek to be aware of when we are doing things for selfish gain.

This, in my mind, is why Jesus was, and continues to be, so influential. *Time* ranked him as the Most Significant Figure in History.[3] He pursued holiness and obedience relentlessly in his life; even his death was in obedience to God and in service to others.

Jack Welch, who grew General Electric's business 4,000 per cent as chairman and CEO between 1981 and 2001, said this: 'Before you are a leader, success is all about growing yourself. When you become a leader, success is all about growing others.'[4]

That's why we started with the five characteristics. By taking responsibility for ourselves, we're trying to make sure, as much as we are able, that the DNA we begin with is as healthy as possible.

And then we seek to nurture those characteristics in others.

Learning from Paul

The apostle Paul was arguably one of the most influential characters in the New Testament.

He had an incredible influence on the early church, which continues to ripple out even to this day. He helped the early Christians grasp both theologically and practically that the death and resurrection of Jesus meant God's kingdom was available to those outside Abraham's family. He saw some extraordinary miracles and was responsible for dozens of church plants in numerous cities. He wrote the majority of the New Testament.

And he also upset people.

Here's the thing: good leadership is about having a positive influence and impact on people's lives, but sometimes being a leader can also create difficult situations.

In Acts 15 there's a disagreement with Barnabas. Barnabas – the guy who, in the early days of Paul's new-found faith, went out of his way to look out for Paul and invest in him; the guy who used his influence to gain Paul an audience with the leaders of the early church; the guy who had been with Paul since the beginning ... The two leaders have different ideas, and disagree so strongly that they have to part company.[5]

As we'll see, leadership is about setting an example, setting the culture, loving and serving others by making decisions. But we're all broken, and sometimes our brokenness clashes with someone else's brokenness and causes more hurt. We need to be careful that we don't do this on purpose (I don't recommend *looking* for disagreements) – but we also need to be honest that, despite how hard we try to reconcile a relationship, sometimes leaders disagree, and our mutual brokenness means it's best for everyone to go our separate ways.

These situations are hard, and can be confusing at times. Paul himself wrote, 'If it is possible, as far as it depends on you, live at peace with everyone.'[6] But sometimes leaders disagree; sometimes pursuing peace means it's necessary to agree to disagree and part ways.

Barnabas and John Mark (the one who the disagreement was all about) headed off in one direction to encourage the churches that had already been planted; Paul went with Silas to do the same in the other direction.

Despite the sadness it can bring, despite knowing that we've done all we can to try to make the relationship work, in those moments we hold on to God's promise, that Paul himself wrote about, that 'in all things God works for the good of those who love him'.[7]

And as Paul started working with Silas, they came across Timothy.

Here's a great story of how God can work things out for good. Timothy would become a really significant part of Paul's team, and his life. Timothy would travel with Paul, learn from him, and eventually go on to be a leader within the church. And Timothy would remain loyal to Paul even when Paul said, 'everyone in the province of Asia has deserted me'.[8]

Paul met Timothy on that first trip after the disagreement with Barnabas.

We read that Timothy's mum, Eunice, became a Christian during Paul's first mission trip, as she and his gran, Lois, heard Paul speaking in the synagogue. And it appears that from then, Timothy started to follow Jesus too.[9]

So Paul invited him to join his team – though the cost was high: his foreskin.

Timothy's mum was Jewish, but his dad was Greek, so he'd never been circumcised. Paul thought it important for Timothy to be identified with the Jewish faith and must have had a really good argument to convince him to go ahead with the circumcision.[10]

(When we planted in Offerton we insisted those planting with us moved into the area. We thought that was a pretty high bar, but Timothy's commitment is on another level.)

From there, we see that Paul and Timothy's relationship flourished in the most wonderful way. Timothy was part of the core team, watching the mission unfold, journeying with Paul through some of the considerable hardships he faced, assisting in planting churches, discussing theology, helping Paul write and deliver some of the letters to churches, and then finally taking on a church of his own to lead and grow, despite his youth.

What was Paul's advice to him, as he was taking on leadership in the church? What's in you ripples out of you; work towards holiness: 'train yourself to be godly. For physical training is of some value, but godliness has value for all things, holding promise for both the present life and the life to come.'[11]

Leading others will create some amazing relationships in which we see individuals thrive. Leading others will also expose our weaknesses like nothing else. If we're going to be successful leaders, we must take responsibility for our own walk with the Lord, and seek to nurture others, having a positive influence in their lives and pointing them towards Jesus.

What are the key areas of weakness and brokenness in you? Has your brokenness ever clashed with someone else's brokenness? After you'd worked through it, can you identify what was your baggage and what was theirs? Was there any transference or projection at play? How did it work out? What might you do differently next time?

And who has led you well? What lessons can you learn from their leadership? How can you do the same for others?

We've seen that leadership means influence (and sometimes disagreements), but as *Christian* leaders we want to do more than simply have a positive impact: we want to influence others towards Jesus. How do we seek to impart his influence into those we lead?

A Non-Anxious Spiritual Resource

A few years ago, I came across the work of Edwin Friedman.

Friedman worked as a family therapist and leadership consultant in all sorts of organisations – both religious and secular – from small families to the US military, helping them work through some of their challenges and dysfunction.

In his book, *A Failure of Nerve*, he argues that the leader in the room is not the person with the power, not the person with the title; but the person with the least amount of *anxiety*.[12]

He came to the conclusion that the best way to address dysfunction was not by trying to work with everyone involved, but to simply invest time in the least anxious person, whatever rank or age they were – because they were the key influencer in their environment. The person who was the non-anxious presence.

I found this fascinating. Through my twenties and thirties I struggled with anxiety and panic attacks. I tended to think I was a pretty relaxed person, but under the surface there was obviously a lot more going on.

If you've ever had a panic attack, you'll know they're awful. Your breathing rate increases, your hands start to sweat, you begin to feel completely out of control. Every sense is heightened, which for me included assessing different aspects of my own physical health, particularly around my brain and my heart. I was terrified of having a brain haemorrhage or a heart attack.

I discovered I had a lot to learn about being the least anxious person in the room.

Add to this the passion both Lizzy and I have for seeing things happen and doing things well. Though this can be admirable, it can also create unhelpful stress and anxiety.

So we've been on a journey of learning to be less anxious, and less stressed, for our own sake, but also for the sake of those around us. Using all the principles we considered in the chapter on growing, Lizzy and I are striving to become more rounded, healthy leaders. We're growing through our frustrations; we're trying to be 'self-differentiated' by not responding to transference or projection;[13] we're choosing to focus on what is both important and urgent, not just urgent; and we're committed to looking after ourselves, our family and our team. By praying, reflecting together and with trusted friends, using Scripture and other helpful resources, and hearing what others say to us, we are trying to grow in peace and emotional health as much as possible. So that we reflect Jesus from the inside out.

I'm not saying we've reached the destination, but we've recognised areas of weakness in ourselves where the Lord wants to work, and we're doing what we can to work on those areas. All with the goal of becoming a non-anxious presence.

But just being a non-anxious presence didn't seem to quite cut it for Lizzy and me. If leaders influence others, they are also using their resources to help and nurture others.

If you're running a company and you're not quite sure what steps to take next, you hire a business consultant – someone who can help determine the goals you want to reach, and how you might get there. If you want to raise some money but are not sure how to do it, you find a fundraiser to help. These people are a resource to you – they are offering leadership in one form or another.

So to be a Christian leader means being a *spiritual* resource to people, pointing them to Jesus. Offering them something from within us, something we have learned from the Lord, or sharing the direction the Lord has called us to walk, and inviting others to join in and journey with us, learn from us, grow with us. Investing what we have into them. That's why our working definition of Christian leadership has become: *a non-anxious spiritual resource.*

The non-anxious and present Christian leader offers a spiritual resource to others – investing in them, helping and nurturing them, directing and enabling them. Pointing them to Jesus, praying with and for them, investing in their spiritual development.

What resources have God and other people invested in you, that you can give away to others? How might you develop your ability to nurture others by becoming a non-anxious spiritual resource to them?

Offering ourselves as a non-anxious spiritual resource to those we are leading means loving and serving them.

#LoveAndServe

The traditional end to an Anglican service is the commissioning, and I love it. 'Go in peace to love and serve the Lord,' says the leader, and everyone responds, 'In the name of Christ, Amen.'

How good is that?

Every person is commissioned, sent out from the place of gathered worship, 'in peace'. Peace with God, peace with ourselves, peace with others. Carriers of peace – a non-anxious presence – in a world craving it. We go with this peace to 'love and serve the Lord', becoming a spiritual resource to others. And we do it all 'in the name of Christ', living as representatives of Jesus. We leave our church gathering, not just to get on with our lives as normal, but to love God and serve him through the week.

It's why the strapline for our church is 'Loving and serving Jesus, each other, Greater Manchester and beyond'. It's why we use the hashtag '#LoveAndServe' in all our social media posts.

We love and serve others in the name of Jesus – the greatest non-anxious spiritual resource to ever walk this planet, and the only one who can help us access true peace, through the presence and power of the Holy Spirit. Through his life he also modelled to us what it means to love and serve others.

Jesus, the ultimate leader and pioneer, taught his disciples this lesson as he washed their feet before the last supper. The story is told in John 13. Consider how extraordinary this is: he knows one of his core team has gone behind his back and betrayed him. He knows all bar one will abandon him out of their own fear and anxieties. He knows he is facing a cruel death. Despite all this, he takes a towel and does the most menial task imaginable. The Teacher, the Rabbi, wrapping a towel around himself and doing the work of someone far below his station.

John 13:3 tells us why he was able to serve his disciples in this profound act of humility: 'Jesus knew that the Father had put all things under his power, and that he had come from God and was returning to God'.

Jesus was so secure in who he was, and his coming vindication, that he was able to offer himself as a non-anxious spiritual resource, even as he approached his betrayal and death. He used his resources to love and serve others. His identity and future were found in the Father's love, and he nurtured others from that place of peace.

When he had finished washing their feet, Jesus asked the Twelve if they understood what he had done for them, and by way of explanation said this:

Now that I, your Lord and Teacher, have washed your feet, you also should wash one another's feet. I have set you an example that you should do as I have done for you. Very truly I tell you, no servant is greater than his master, nor is a messenger greater than the one who sent him. Now that you know these things, you will be blessed if you do them.[14]

The point of all that we do as followers of Jesus is not to prove how good we are. The point of planting or pioneering is not to show others that our idea or vision was right. That would be planting for *our* sake.

The point is to serve others. Planting for the sake of others.

I'm not saying there won't be mixed motives within us – we all want to succeed, or at least be seen to be successful. The challenge is to not allow that to come first. First comes our desire to serve the Lord, serve his people and serve those who don't yet know him. When that doesn't come first, the correct response is repentance – changing our perspective, admitting where our hearts are astray from the ideal and asking God to help us put first things first.

To delegate well is to serve the person to whom we're handing over responsibility. We want the best for them and to do what we can for their success. As we look to multiply, and delegate tasks and responsibilities, are we doing it for the sake of the person we're delegating to, or for our own sake? Unless we are serving others in our delegating, people might rightly get the impression we're just using them to get things off our plate that we don't want to do ourselves.

Come on, let's be really honest with each other for a moment. This pioneering thing, are you doing it for you, or for others? Allow the Holy Spirit to point out to you the places where you're doing it for yourself. He's not surprised by it. He's just keen that we're aware of our own brokenness and pride so that we can keep bringing it to him, dying to ourselves and living to Christ.

Becoming free to love and serve others.

Set an Example

Jesus loved and served his disciples by modelling what he wanted, and explaining what he was doing – leading by example. It seems we can't expect things to be a priority for the people we lead if they are not a priority for us.

For instance, this means that before we can lead others in praying, we need to have something of a prayer life, a pattern of prayer, that we can invite people into.

Eugene Peterson argues that the work of a pastor is to preach and to pray: to offer our people an example of what it means to follow Jesus through our words and our lives.[15] Our emotional, physical and spiritual health will have an impact on the community which develops around us.

That's why, each week, Lizzy and I gather with our staff team to give space for each team member to share what's going well and what's hard – not just in ministry, but in life. We share and pray together so we can grow together. Each month we gather with our small group leaders, and we share and pray together in a similar way.

I mentioned in the chapter on prayer that when we planted in Stockport I took some time each morning at 9 a.m. to pray and worship. It was a pattern I wanted to see develop in the life of the church we were planting, so I took the lead. I did myself what I wanted to see develop as we grew.

Within a couple of years, we had taken on the drop-in centre and a couple of staff, some interns and a number of volunteers. So each morning, before opening, we would gather at 9 a.m. in Glo Central for half an hour to worship and pray.

We used morning prayer as our guide.[16] (It's humbling to remember that we're not the first ones with a good idea; the church has been worshipping and praying together first thing in the morning for millennia!) We sang some songs, read the set Scriptures for the day, and prayed for the issues going on around us.

If you came to our church now – a totally different church in a totally different context – you'd find us doing the same thing. Why? Because what's in the leader gets replicated in the church.

What's your pattern of prayer? How will it be replicated in the community of faith you are pioneering? And what about the four other characteristics? How do you set an example around envisioning? What repeatable practices or easy language can you give people to help model and explain what you're longing to see? And what about setting an example in growing? Acting? Learning?

Set the Culture

By setting an example – by modelling and explaining – we begin to set a culture. So we need to be really thoughtful about what we do with our time and energy.

Lizzy loves things tidy and ordered – it's a key strategy she uses as someone with dyslexia to try to keep things sorted in a busy mind. One particular Sunday, as we were setting up for worship, I couldn't work out where Lizzy was or what she was doing. Eventually we found her in the toddlers' toy store, frustrated about the mess in which it had been left and trying to sort it all out.

People were arriving for the gathering, and instead of being available to welcome as they came in, Lizzy was stressed and frustrated, sorting out a cupboard, and I was stressed and frustrated that she was clearing a cupboard instead of helping set things up for the service. In different ways, we were both unavailable physically or emotionally to others. Hardly a loving atmosphere for people to walk into.

As we reflected later that day, we realised we were both doing what we considered important and urgent tasks, but that the most important role as leaders is to help set the tone as people arrive to worship the Lord: welcome people, pastor people, connect newcomers to people who could sit with them, love and serve them. Instead, we were both getting on with activities that made people feel less important than the jobs we were doing.

Eugene Peterson suggests that there are two types of connection between people: *communication* and *communion*.[17] Communication is when information is shared – notices, plans, times, dates. You might say it's the head stuff. But communion is where we share our hearts: how we're doing, what's going on in us right now – heart-to-heart connection.

Part of setting culture is being aware of the needs of those around you – so as leaders, we need to think carefully about how and when we share what's on our own hearts. Mike Breen, who was the leader of our church in Sheffield, used the analogy of a seesaw in a children's playground: when the team or church are doing well, they're up, and you can be a little more honest about places where you're struggling. But when they're down, it's your job as the leader to be up – to model thankfulness to God, faith and trust in him. (You'll still need to find places where you can be transparent and vulnerable, but that's not always with the people following you.)

Communication and communion. Modelling and explaining. Seeing where your team is at and assessing how appropriate it is to share what's going on with you. All of this takes *time*. To be present with people as they are walking into a meeting means you've spent enough time preparing so that you're not scurrying around in a great rush (or busy in a cupboard!).

To be a non-anxious spiritual resource to others means giving them enough time with you for your resources to be available to them. In some seasons, Lizzy and I have done this well. In other, busier seasons, it can be much harder.

If culture is both modelled and explained, you could say it gets both *caught* and *taught*. We need to be proactive as leaders in explaining the things that are most important to us, so that others understand the why, as well as the what and how. That's how it gets taught. But it gets caught by allowing people access to our lives so they can see how that works itself out for us.

One of the best ways to offer access to our lives is by sharing food with others – offering the gift of hospitality, where people see your home, see your family relationships, see how it really works out in practice. In the chapter on growing, I described how we do 'please and thank yous' at breakfast and 'highs and lows' at dinner. Guests join in. It's one of the simple ways we try to share our family culture with those who join us – turning towards God in a fun, non-religious way as we share a meal together.[18]

Yet as we invite others in and share our culture with them, there will be some who don't get it or don't want to fit within it.

Jesus himself experienced this. John 6 records him teaching about being the bread of life, and it was proving divisive. Everyone loved it when he had fed the five thousand. Now they weren't so sure, and 'From this time many of his disciples turned back and no longer followed him'.[19] Sometimes setting the culture in a certain way means some people don't feel like they fit, and they turn away.

What did Jesus do? He asked the Twelve if they wanted to leave him too. But they made the choice to stay, and so Jesus continued to invest in them.

Like Deborah's experience of calling on the tribes, sometimes we just have to make the most of those who are willing to step up and serve, rather than get too frustrated about those who say no. The Lord is able to use those who work with you to bring about his purposes, even if it's fewer than you would like. Jesus continued to invest in the Twelve, despite knowing one of them would betray him. Leadership isn't always easy, or fun.

How have you seen other leaders positively set the culture of a team? What kind of team culture are you aiming for? Who has God given you to work with?

Stories Nurture Culture

If we want to lead churches full of people who are confident in stepping out in faith (our language for this is '*a community of radical disciples of Jesus*'), this too starts with us. Stories of what God is doing inspire others to be hungry for similar stories, so sharing testimonies of what

God is doing in and through you is a crucial way to grow faith in others. Similarly, hearing stories from other people in the church – not just the leaders, but others who have seen God at work – can be hugely encouraging.

I've heard it said: what you celebrate, you propagate.

The saints are celebrated in Revelation because they triumphed over Satan 'by the blood of the Lamb and by the word of their testimony'.[20] Jesus has won the victory for us through his death and resurrection, but testimony is a powerful weapon: reminding ourselves and each other of what God has done for us, and what God has done through us.

In 2019, our family had the privilege of visiting Jackie Pullinger in Hong Kong. Lizzy and I both read her book *Chasing the Dragon* when we were teenagers, and it had a profound effect on us. But Lizzy (who was inspired to spend her life serving society's most vulnerable after reading it) was particularly excited. We were so grateful to be able to go and learn from her and others who had seen Jesus transform people's lives – from being involved in gangs and drugs to becoming healed, whole people, set free to be all God made them to be.

As we talked with and served alongside her and the team, we heard stories from some of the people whose lives had been transformed. Stories that inspired and challenged us. Stories that lifted our faith. Stories that opened our eyes even more fully to what Jesus can do.

Jackie suggested to us that the best way to encourage our people as we returned home was to tell stories that make people jealous for what we had seen, and hungry for more of Jesus.

The simple power of testimony.

As we told stories of all we had seen Jesus do in Hong Kong, we saw people inspired and challenged, just as we had been. People's faith began to rise, just as ours had done. People's eyes were opened more to all that Jesus can and wants to do.

If we don't step out and do things, though, we won't have stories. If we wait for everything to be perfect, or until we have enough confidence to do something without any fear, we'll never do anything.

Leading others means making decisions, taking responsibility, loving and serving by setting the example, and creating the culture through choosing what gets celebrated.

Paul's advice to Timothy, when he was a young leader wanting to lead in the best way possible, was to 'set an example for the believers in speech, in conduct, in love, in faith and in purity'.[21]

How can you use stories to help set the culture of thanksgiving and faith?

Leaders Intentionally Pour into Others

If we're going to see what God has placed in us ripple out into the lives of those around us, then we need to carefully think about how we can intentionally pour into others what God has poured into us. Back in the chapter on learning, we looked at the disciples' relationship with Jesus to consider how *we* learn. The same process can be useful in reflecting on how we help *others* learn.

I Do, You Watch

Jesus was already preaching, already healing, when he invited Peter and Andrew to join him: 'Come, follow me.'[22] They didn't do much initially, other than watch and learn. He modelled to them what he wanted them to do – he set the example. Lizzy encouraged me in evangelism by showing me how she did it. She did what she did naturally, and tried to explain afterwards how she was doing it and why. Modelling and explaining, caught and taught.

At this stage, those you are leading will have good levels of vision and excitement, but they're only just beginning to understand what you're doing and why. In the theory of teaching, learners at this stage are referred to as being 'unconsciously incompetent' – they don't know what they don't know. So leading others in this stage requires balancing their considerable passion and excitement with their lack of knowledge or capability.

What do you want people to learn from you? When you're planting a new church or ministry, what skills do you want your team to learn? How are you going to create the space for them to be around you, in order that they can watch?

I Do, You Help

Leading through this stage involves giving someone a chance to join in with something you're doing. Jesus taught from Peter's boat, and then got the disciples to go fishing, where he provided a great catch of fish.[23] He did it, they helped. They had no idea how he did it, but he got them involved.

Just like the time I referred to in the chapter on learning, when a guy let me help set up the sound equipment. I became 'consciously incompetent' – I was increasingly aware of all that I didn't know. At this stage, enthusiasm can wane, frustrations can kick in, and it can feel easier to just find another exciting vision – like so many did in John 6.

As we noted, again in the chapter on learning, when the disciples were freaking out, Jesus said to them, 'Do not be afraid, little flock, for your Father has been pleased to give you the kingdom.'[24] He reminded them of the vision, and loved them through it.

When you're developing your team, how can they be involved so it's not just you doing stuff, but them joining in? What can they do with you? And when things get tough for them, how can you nurture them with love and vision?

You Do, I Help

Here's where we start to delegate responsibility as well as tasks, where we are leading people through the stage of being 'consciously competent'. Like a learner driving a car, they are focusing really hard on everything they have learned, but it doesn't quite feel natural yet. Your job is to encourage them, support them – but also to coach them and challenge them:

Remember what we said?
You did that really well.
What would you do differently next time?
Do you recall how I tried to do it?

Supporting and challenging as we delegate and entrust.

Just like Jesus, asking the disciples to feed the crowd of thousands.[25]
You've seen me trust the Father. You've seen amazing miracles. I'm here to support you, but am challenging you to do it instead of me. He was there to help when they didn't know what to do, but supported and challenged them to grow in their leadership.

As a leader, are you better at offering support or challenge? Your team are going to need both, and most of us are better at one than the other. So you're going to need to learn to delegate responsibility (that's hard enough in itself), and then offer both support and challenge to your team.

You Do, I Watch

Unconsciously competent. That's the dream. That people unconsciously get the culture you're setting, the way you do things, why you do them that way, how they are done well ...

I'm not encouraging us to develop minions or carbon copies of ourselves; I'm saying that every driving instructor gets excited when their student passes their test and can drive without them. Those you lead will develop their own 'driving' style, which will reflect your teaching, but they'll be confident in the basics and develop from there.

Paul is bold enough to say to the church in Corinth: 'imitate me'.[26] And then he explains why he has sent Timothy: 'He will remind you of my way of life in Christ Jesus, which agrees with what I teach everywhere in every church.'[27]

I trust him. He gets it. He's become unconsciously competent in this stuff, and I'm completely confident in entrusting this job to him.

Like Jesus, commissioning his disciples. *You've been with me, you've learned this stuff from me, now go and do the same for others.*[28]

Just because someone is unconsciously competent doesn't mean they don't need to learn anymore. Goran Ivanišević doesn't need to teach Novak Djokovic how to play tennis. Djokovic is unconsciously competent. But his coach helps him become conscious of little tweaks he could make to continue to improve.

Jesus promised the Holy Spirit would be with us through all these stages as we step out and lead – we are not on our own: 'the Advocate, the Holy Spirit, whom the Father will send in my name, will teach you all things and will remind you of everything I have said to you'.[29]

So with the Holy Spirit's help and guidance, aware of our weaknesses but convinced of God's call, and encouraged by others, building the five characteristics into our own lives, we step out and start to lead. Leading others is about being a non-anxious spiritual resource who loves and serves, setting an example and a culture where those we lead are nurtured into becoming unconsciously competent leaders in their own right.

And from there, it begins to ripple out.

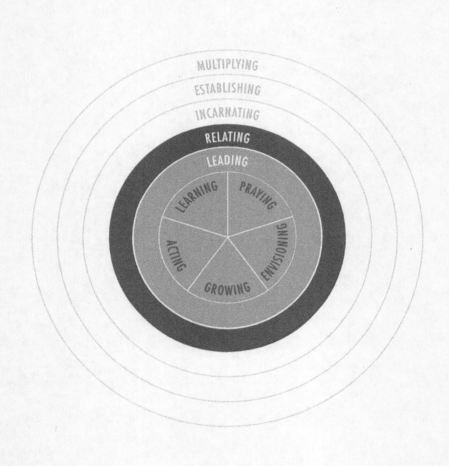

7

Relating

People. That's what pioneering and planting is all about, because that's what the kingdom of God is all about: seeing people step out of darkness into light.

So if the kingdom of God is about people, then it's about relationships. And although I don't like hierarchical language, it can be helpful to recognise that, as church planters, there are four different categories of people we're in relationship with:

'Above' you: relationships with those to whom you are accountable – those who are sending, funding and rooting for you – the people in your *supporting organisations*.

'Alongside' you: relationships with people on the ground, working in that context already – the people in *other agencies*.

'Below' you: relationships with those who might join you to fulfil the vision – your *team*.

'Beyond' you: relationships with those you are trying to reach – the people in your *context*.

It looks like this:

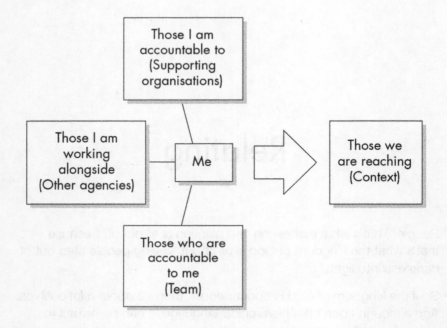

We'll discuss in the next chapter on incarnating how we build relationships with the people we are trying to reach. But let's start by looking at how we develop relationships with those in the other three categories. As pioneers and planters, it's our job to relate well to all these people and organisations. So, how do we do that? How do we keep it all in balance, while keeping the main thing the main thing: seeing new people enter the kingdom of God?

Building Team

Let's start by looking at those who will join you: those in your team. Once again, the apostle Paul is a great example for us.

Paul didn't work alone. In Acts 11 we read that Barnabas had been sent to Antioch to teach and encourage the new church which had been planted there. He then decided to find Saul (who had hunkered down in Tarsus and changed his name to Paul) and bring him to Antioch, where together they taught the church. A year later, they were worshipping with some other believers when there was a prophetic word to send the two of them off on mission.[1]

The two of them were sent out to see what God would do. But they also brought along their friend John, to be 'with them as their helper'.[2]

In fact, Paul was always working with someone else, and as we saw in the previous chapter on leading, by Acts 16 he was travelling with Timothy and Luke, along with Silas, his new co-worker. In each place, they raised up new leaders.

Team is key when we're planting. You don't need a huge team, but when you're alone, you're what Derek Sivers calls a 'lone nut'.[3] When you're doing something on your own, the work might not appear particularly credible; but when someone else joins you they demonstrate their commitment to you, and it offers a model to others of what it means to participate in what you are doing. It creates a sense of validity – someone else has bought into the vision: this is something worth joining.

Sivers says, 'The first follower transforms a lone nut into a leader.'[4] Lots of people have good ideas. Some of those people begin to put their ideas into practice. Leaders help others see and understand their ideas and get them involved.

So how do we know who to choose to be part of our team?

Understanding your strengths within the fivefold ministries in Ephesians 4 can be really helpful; discerning whether you are primarily an apostle, prophet, evangelist, pastor or teacher can help you determine your own areas of strength and weakness.[5] It can also help you identify the gaps, and the kinds of people you need to look for when recruiting a team. Planters and pioneers often tend to be apostolic types and are therefore not always gifted in pastoral work, so two things are needed: the first is to try to learn some of the skills a natural pastor takes for granted; the second is to look for someone who is gifted as a pastor to be part of the team.

Trying to understand how different people tick, by using tools such as Myers-Briggs, DiSC, Belbin, Enneagram and other personality tests can also really help (though not all at the same time!).[6]

However, assuming that you can simply recruit a great team by looking just for a primary gifting or personality type is to misunderstand how the Lord works.

Jesus carefully chose the Twelve and invited them to 'Follow me'. It took him time, prayer and reflection. Think about the team he called: fishermen; a tax collector who had been in league with the Romans; a zealot who had been fighting *against* the Romans ... A rag-tag group of people that, humanly speaking, made no sense at all. Perhaps not all of them were the obvious first choice, but prayer can do that. When we connect with God's heart in prayer, we begin to see people and their potential from God's point of view, rather than just our own.

Gathering good people around you is crucial. Lizzy and I have been blessed to work with some amazing people who've joined us on our teams. We wouldn't be the people we are today, and we wouldn't have done the things we've done, if it wasn't for those who joined us in what God was calling us to do.

One of the most helpful tools we've used when team building is derived from Bill Hybels' '3 Cs' of team building: character, calling, competence and chemistry (yes, there are four. We added 'calling').[7]

Character

Character is to do with the kind of person we are, rather than the things we do. Character is saying yes and doing it; stickability and faithfulness in the midst of things being hard; honesty and integrity.

When I was a worship leader, I used to teach that character is more important than gifting – you can have the greatest electric guitarist in the world, but if they consistently turn up late to rehearsal, nursing a hangover, they're not really in the right place to be leading others in worship.

Think about it like this. Let's say, when my kids were young, I gave one of them a gift – maybe an art set, or a tricycle. What would I want them to do with it? I'd want them to start using the paint brushes, or have a go riding the tricycle. I wouldn't give them the gift so they could show off with it: *look at my pens; isn't my trike amazing?* I would give it to them so they would learn how to use it. I wouldn't be impressed with the gift itself, because I was the one who gave it to them!

This is the trouble with us finding our sense of security in our gifting – we try to impress God and others with the things we are naturally gifted at, but the Lord is looking for us to use the gifts he has given in the service of him and others. That's what demonstrates and develops character.

Do those you are considering to be part of your team demonstrate good character? Do they use their gifts to serve God and others?

It takes time to determine character – you can't do it in a short conversation or an hour-long interview. (I've heard it said that 'any donkey can look like a racehorse for an hour'!) When you're thinking about whether or not to invite someone onto your team, it can be helpful to seek others' opinion of the individual. Are they a person of character? Would those who know them better want them on their team?

Calling

As you consider character – humbly recognising there is no perfect person, just as you are not – you also consider calling. You want to know that the individual senses God's call to join your team. And you, as their leader, also want to be able to affirm that calling.

Gideon, as he reluctantly stepped into leadership, had an interesting problem.[8] Although lots of people responded to his call to arms, many of them were fearful, and when he gave them the opportunity to go back home, they took up the offer.

Over two-thirds of them. Twenty-two thousand people, leaving just ten thousand.

You know the rest of the story – from there, the Lord whittled them down to Israel's own version of *the three hundred*.[9]

It doesn't always make sense to say 'no' in the natural, but it does in the spiritual. God wasn't looking for the biggest team for Gideon; he was looking for a way to bring glory to himself through just a small group of people.

When Lizzy and I have been building team, we've often asked people to be sure that God is calling them to join us. The reason for this is simple: if you're responding merely to a human invitation, then when things go wrong (and they will) and when things get hard (and they will), someone can legitimately come to us and say, 'This is not what you promised or told us would happen.' The responsibility to fix it is on us.

However, if the Lord is calling you, then when things go wrong (and they will) and when things get hard (and they will), we can all go to the Lord together and say, 'Lord, what are you up to? This is not what we expected. Show us what you're trying to do or say.'

Remember, the Lord uses our journey to teach us, discipline us, grow us. We're interested in the destination; he's interested in how we get there.

Gideon just wanted to win. God wanted to demonstrate his glory.

Do those you are inviting to join your team sense God's call? Releasing really good people to hear God for themselves, rather than trying to convince them to join you, is hard. But giving them the opportunity to do so is worth it in the long run.

And for those who want to join your team, do you as their leader sense they are called too? Make sure not only that they believe God is calling them to join you; make sure *you* believe it too, otherwise it's going to be really hard for you to lead them and engage with them fully.

Competence

I used to say I was looking for 'character, not gifting'. It was a good bit of hyperbole to make a point.

But I realised I was wrong.

A better phrase is 'character *before* gifting'. If you're putting together a worship team, then it turns out gifting is quite important – you don't want someone in your worship team who can't make the right chord shapes.

Competence is important – if you're looking for someone in your team who might be good at working with kids, then that's a valid skill to be searching for.

Or maybe you need a treasurer, like we did when we planted into central Manchester. We inherited a congregation of about fifteen people, most of whom were on the church council. And it turned out that the books weren't up to date. No money was being laundered and no profiteering was going on – these were good people who were doing their best to try to keep the church open. But we needed some help.

Our prayer became really specific: 'Lord, we need someone to help with the finances.'

One Sunday, in through the door walks a couple who joined us having just handed on a church they planted to other leaders. And it turned out that the guy had a background in finances.

He understood finances, and he was a church planter!

John helped us enormously in our first couple of years, getting our books up to date, and helping with the budget and other financial processes.

We desperately needed someone who was competent in finance, and the Lord graciously provided.

What kind of gifting are you looking for in your team? How much are you willing to invest in someone to get them up to speed? What compromises are you willing to make, and where do you need to stand firm?

Chemistry

We all have people with whom we click. People we enjoy hanging out with, people who make us laugh, people we look forward to seeing with eager anticipation. That's what chemistry looks like.

So when considering team members, you're looking for people you might enjoy spending time with, through the good times and the bad.

That's not to say you're just looking for people who are like you – that doesn't build a great team.

When we planted Saint Philips Chapel Street, we intentionally tried to recruit a staff member from a minority background, so our church more accurately represented the place where we were planting. I asked some leaders I respected from a different ethnic background if they knew of anyone we could employ for one day a week (it's all we could afford) to lead and develop our work with students. We were looking for someone different to us – and when we met Lizzie, there was a chemistry which meant that though our ethnicities and backgrounds were very different, we knew we could work together. She's awesome: she loves the Lord, has a powerful testimony of God's work in her life, and she got the vision. She had the character, the calling, the competence *and* the chemistry.

But we've also had to say no to some people joining our team, on the basis of chemistry. It was just a gut feeling, and these conversations rank in my 'Top Ten Most Awkward Conversations Ever'. But I'm so glad I had them.

One person comes to mind who had some good competencies; they definitely felt called, and they served well in their church, demonstrating character. But our gut feeling when we met with them was 'no'. We didn't see how they could form part of our core team. They had the right heart, they served well, but there wasn't the same chemistry we had when we met with our student worker Lizzie, for example. We also couldn't see this person fitting with the others we'd gathered as team – team meetings would be awkward, polite, difficult. That's not what we wanted for our planting team, and so I went to speak to them and explained that although we appreciated they sensed a call to join us, we weren't sure about it. There were some family issues they were facing, and I didn't think a church-planting team was the right place to deal with those.

They took it really badly.

I felt awful. They had been so excited; they had been willing to move house, do all the things we were asking the planting team to do. But the chemistry wasn't there. And in time, it became clear that they wouldn't have been the right fit in our church plant.

Is there chemistry between you and the person wanting to join your team? Are you willing to have the honest conversations now, to avoid the more difficult ones in the future?

Trust your gut. Don't just build a team with people who are like you. But do build team with those the Lord is giving you peace about, and don't be afraid to say no.

Finding Team

Probably the number one question people ask about planting and pioneering is 'Where can I *find* team?' 'Where do the people come from to join me?' These questions aren't about *how* to gather people, but *where* to gather them from. The reality is that finding and building team takes time and effort.

It starts in prayer. 'Lord, who are you putting on my mind and heart to invite? If you're in this, then there must be some others who get it too and want to join in. Who are they, Lord?'

And then, envision people. Ask everyone.

Start with the obvious – your friends, those closest to you. Most plants have a donor church, which should be an easy place from which to gather team if they are being envisioned about planting already (although relationship with your donor church needs to be done well too – we'll look more into this later).

When we planted Saint Philips Chapel Street, we didn't have a mother church – Lizzy and I were leading Glo and didn't want to take anyone from there with us. We wanted to see the leaders and the church at Glo succeed and go on without us, but it meant we had to find team from other places.

So we started with the team we could employ – our first curate and worship leader, and our youth and kids worker. They were great people who we knew through New Wine, and so we extended an invitation for them to join us. We continued to connect with people through all the networks we had, and held some vision nights, where people could come and hear about what we were doing.

We worked connection after connection: *so-and-so knows so-and-so who might be interested … great, let's get some time with them.* Build relationships. Share the vision.

A few joined us, many didn't. So we started with twenty-three – fourteen adults and nine children.

The key is to ask everybody, and to use the five characteristics we talked about in the first half of the book, even in your team building. *Pray* for the right people. Share your *vision* with everyone you meet – remember the thirty-second version, five-minute version, and thirty-minute version of the vision, and share it with people, inviting them into it. Allow the process to *grow* you as a disciple of Jesus, in humility, in trust, in holiness. *Act* – you don't build team by sitting around waiting for it to happen. And *learn* – what went well? What did people respond positively to? Could I have shared that better?

One guy I know wanted to recruit some more team members, so he created a YouTube video sharing his vision, which he posted online. He sat waiting and hoping someone would watch the video and come to join him. But it didn't work: nobody joined. Finding team is not just about vision, it's to do with relationships, networking with people and building a shared sense of call with others.

Let's face it, if people are going to join you to start a new church, they need to trust you. They need to trust God is calling them into it, especially if it means selling their house and buying a new one, finding new schools for their kids and possibly even finding a new job. Trust can be given, not just earned, but relationship is key in the building of trust, and therefore in the building of team.

Who could you ask? Who knows people who might know people? Can you give your vision in thirty seconds?

Healthy Team

Once you've got your first followers – those who've captured something of the vision and sensed God's call to join you – start to walk through the five characteristics with them. This, remember, is what ripples out of you, into them, and beyond them into the community you're trying to reach.

As the team grows and therefore relationships grow, you need to work at building those relationships to be as strong as possible.

It would be great if we could live in harmony the whole time. The problem is, we're all human, we all miss the mark and we all let people down.

So, to help us grow healthy relationships, we talk about 'doing Matthew 18'.

Matthew 18 is Jesus' brilliant way of restoring relationships in a mature way. So, we've turned some verses in which Jesus taught about dealing with sin into a core team value.

> If your brother or sister sins, go and point out their fault, just between the two of you. If they listen to you, you have won them over. But if they will not listen, take one or two others along, so that 'every matter may be established by the testimony of two or three witnesses.' If they still refuse to listen, tell it to the church; and if they refuse to listen even to the church, treat them as you would a pagan or a tax collector.[10]

Before we dive in and look in more detail, a couple of caveats.

First, this should never be used to blame-shift. We've discussed holiness and humility at length already, but it needs to be mentioned here again, because if applied incorrectly, Matthew 18 can be used to put the responsibility on others rather than examining our own motives and behaviours. 'Go and point out their fault' can too easily turn into, 'Blame someone else when things aren't right'.

Jesus said in the Sermon on the Mount, 'Why do you look at the speck of sawdust in your brother's eye and pay no attention to the plank in your own eye?'[11] In the same passage, he told us not to judge, and that the measure we use to judge others is the measure that will be used against us[12] – clearly an encouragement for self-reflection not blame-shifting. Jesus also established the rule of love: 'A new command I give you: love one another.'[13]

Applying Matthew 18 is more difficult when there's a power dynamic involved. Even though you might not *feel* particularly powerful, as the team leader you have leadership responsibility; you're in charge. And this may make it more challenging for someone within your church to confront you – especially if they are staff, and their job depends on you. So, if you need to follow Matthew 18 with someone in your team or church, just remember the power dynamic: you as their leader confronting them is not the same as a peer confronting them.

The best leaders recognise their own brokenness and try to deal with it by growing, not by projecting their issues onto others – it's all too easy to blame others and assume it's 'their issue'. We convince ourselves that we're right and someone else is wrong[14] – when more often than not there has been a misunderstanding, a miscommunication, which is much better resolved by *asking*, rather than *accusing*. (Just take a minute to remember who, in Scripture, has the title 'the accuser' …

Exactly.)

Second, following this process, especially Step 1, can be harmful rather than helpful in cases where abuse of some kind is brought into the light. Those who've been abused do not need to face their abuser. I believe Matthew 18 is about having an honest conversation in what feels like a safe environment for both parties.

So, using the rule of love; making sure we take the log out of our own eye before approaching someone to address their speck; and asking not accusing, let's get into it.

Step 1

'If your brother or sister sins, go and point out their fault, just between the two of you. If they listen to you, you have won them over.'

If someone misses the mark, or lets you down, or you spot they're up to something no good, don't put it on social media, and don't go around behind their backs talking to everybody else about it – that's gossip. Go to the person, and and ask them about it. Remember, don't accuse, ask. Assuming you've misunderstood is a good, humble way in.

If someone comes to us, as leaders, with an issue they're having with another person, or a concern they might have about someone, our first question is always the same: 'Have you talked to them about it?' If the answer is 'no', then that's the first thing they need to do.

If they come to us with a problem they have with us, then of course that's difficult, but we're grateful they came to speak to us about it rather than going behind our backs. These can be hard conversations, but they are part of a significant growth process for all involved.

Step 2

'But if they will not listen, take one or two others along, so that "every matter may be established by the testimony of two or three witnesses."'

If that first conversation didn't resolve things, share the situation with a few trusted friends – not as gossip, but as a chance to pray and reflect and then try the conversation again. Preferably, these friends would have in some way witnessed the issue that needs resolving; but they can be character witnesses for both perspectives. What you don't want is to whip up a few people to see things from your perspective and come down hard together on the person in question – and neither do you want people who loyally defend their leader, no matter what. Instead, those you ask to be involved should help to create a further conversation, in which both sides are considered and both perspectives are taken into account. Ultimately, any sin should be named and called out for what it is, so that forgiveness can be offered and received both ways, and relationship restored.

Step 3

'If they still refuse to listen, tell it to the church ...'

Bring it to 'the church'. I don't think this means during Sunday worship! My understanding of this is that it relates to a larger group than in the last step, including some trusted and wise elders, who can help discern the situation together. By listening to both sides, by praying and offering their wisdom, the aim here again is to create a context for reflection, repentance and reconciliation.

Step 4

'... and if they refuse to listen even to the church, treat them as you would a pagan or a tax collector.'

If they are unrepentant, unwilling to change or admit any wrongdoing, then you still have to forgive them, but treat them as if they are outside the church, not inside. There are consequences to our actions when we're in community, and the community itself needs to work out how it deals with activity that could be harmful; recognising power dynamics, working within the rule of love, the Sermon on the Mount, and through asking not accusing.

But, there's still a note of grace here: how did Jesus treat pagans and tax collectors? He loved them, spent time with them and shared the gospel with them.

Following Matthew 18 is a really helpful way of learning to deal with disagreements and misunderstandings. If church is family, then it's all about relationships, which means it's all about communication, and communication can sometimes go wrong. So we need short accounts with each other, and walking through this process helps with that.

And man, it helps you grow! I knew of one leader who viewed

confrontation as a spiritual discipline. This is a good way of thinking about it – as a way to help us grow, first through self-reflection, and then if necessary by humbly asking and working through issues with others. Yes, it's so hard. It would be so much easier to vent my spleen over the internet, or get a group around me who agree that I'm right and they're wrong. But Jesus wants more for us than that, and doesn't allow us to treat anyone as an object without the dignity of loving them.

Support *and* Challenge

Here's something worth pondering: confrontation does not need to be *confrontational*.

As in, you don't have to be all 'alpha male or female' about challenging someone.

As leaders, it's inevitable there'll be times when we have to confront others around attitudes or behaviours. But, part of growing is learning to confront with kindness and humility. In fact, I would argue that confrontation without kindness and humility is dangerous. (I'm speaking from personal experience, having been on both the receiving and giving end, and seeing the consequences – which are often not pretty.)

Confrontation must always be for the good of the other, which means we have to do the hard work within ourselves first.

And challenge must always come alongside support. The person we are confronting needs to know that we love them.

I once had a team member who was on staff at the church but was underperforming. I planned time to work out the particular issues I wanted to raise with him, and took him out to lunch. Throughout the lunch I gently worked my way through the issues I wanted to address, and we resolved ways to help him be more productive.

My final issue was that I wanted him to be able to confront others on his team who were also underperforming. He told me how much he hated being confrontational. And I talked him through our conversation over lunch. 'Did you think this was confrontational?' I asked him. 'No,' he admitted. We can confront with support and kindness, but only if we are willing to do the confrontation with humility, doing the hard work within ourselves so that we are taking the log out of our own eye before trying to help others take the speck out of theirs.[15]

One of my leaders said that confrontation is like a spiritual discipline. It's not easy, and it has to do its work on you first, before you speak to the other person about it. We're not in the blame game; we're in the relationship game. So let's do all we can to avoid being the kind of hypocrite Jesus described in Matthew 7:5.

How does challenging others make you feel? Are you willing to allow the Holy Spirit to do the internal work on you before you go and confront others? Can you model what it means to confront with kindness and humility? We only learn this stuff by giving it a go and trying to improve at it.

Beyond Team

Alongside relating to the team, you will also be relating to people at the various organisations we mentioned at the start of the chapter.

Like I said, I don't really like hierarchical language, but the reality is, there are people and organisations 'above' you – to whom you're accountable. There are people 'alongside' you – with whom you could partner. And there are people 'below' you – those accountable to you, the people you're leading.

We've already looked into building team, so let's consider the organisations alongside you. These are the charities, businesses, social agencies and others who are already at work in the community. When we planted both Glo Church and Saint Philips Chapel Street, we went with the intention of 'not stepping on anyone's toes'. If someone was already doing something great in the community, we didn't want to come in and start competing.

Planting a church can be intimidating for other churches, especially ones who have been around for a long time but are struggling or weak for one reason or another. Even though that's not your responsibility, they are still brothers and sisters in the kingdom, and it's important to honour, rather than ignore, what's going on already.

When we started Glo, the bishop had already identified there wasn't much going on at all. But through our relationship with the council, which I described in the chapter on envisioning, we were invited to some significant meetings where all the stakeholders working in the area would come together, share what they were doing, as well as best practice, and try to support one another.

Previous experience had taught us that councils could be pretty resistant to the work of Christians. But not here – they were so grateful for all we were doing, and wanted to cheer us on. It meant creating time to go to these meetings, which – if I'm honest – didn't always feel necessary for what we were trying to do.

But that's my point.

The meetings allowed the time to build relationships, and it meant that we became trusted by other agencies, rather than treated as suspicious. When a key council worker experienced a tragedy, she came to us to help her process it, pray through it, and write a prayer for her friend's funeral.

We were cautious, however, in not wanting to just be seen by the community as another agency. We were different, because we lived in the local area. We didn't go home to another place, but went home down the road, within the community. Many people distrusted the council, police and social workers; they represented agencies who did things *to* them.

We wanted to be church *with* them, not just a service *for* them.

It was a game changer.

When we planted in central Manchester, Lizzy started connecting with vulnerable women involved in the sex industry, and she went to visit a local charity to get their wisdom and hear how she could work together with them. They had provided support to female sex workers for twenty-five years, and yet Lizzy was the first person from any church in recent memory who'd asked to meet with them. Having heard about what we were trying to do, and having built trust with Lizzy, they then referred women to the church for us to support them.

Similarly, when Pete Hughes planted KXC in London, he decided that the church wouldn't start any of their own social action projects for the first year or so, but instead encouraged people to get involved in local charities. The charities knew the local area and the local needs, so it made sense to get involved, cheer them on, build relationships and get to know the community.

It takes time, but trust flows through relationship, and building those relationships takes investment. Sometimes sitting in meetings can feel pointless (and it's worth regularly reviewing how we spend our time) but often the meetings provide the context to grow rapport.

It can feel like there are any number of things we could be doing that are more urgent, but sometimes the relationship is more important.

If this is true for those we work alongside, it's just as true for those we work under – those to whom we are accountable.

After planting Glo Church, I would write a newsletter and send it out every month to the mother church and those who committed to pray or give to support our work. I would also send it to the bishop. A couple of years in, when we had been successful in some funding applications, I had to write updates for those agencies too.

We were accountable to them because of the investment they made in us.

Honestly, there were many times when I felt I could have been using my time better. I could have been connecting with the people in need around me, doing something more 'useful'. But, as with working alongside others, it takes time to invest in the relationships with those to whom you are accountable. And it's rarely wasted time.

The updates served as a real encouragement to others: their investment was having an impact; it was worth the bishop taking the risk; it was worth the mother church redirecting some finances towards this mission; the prayers of many were being answered. And the updates encouraged us too – *look at all the Lord is doing and has done!*

Ian Parkinson, who led our mother church All Saints Marple, reminded me that bishops very rarely get good news. They have to deal with all sorts of problems and disgruntled people who think they should do this, that or the other.

After Ian's prompting, I resolved to try to become the good news guy.

Trust Accounts

I'm sure you've heard of 'trust accounts' – how relationships work like a bank account, in which you make deposits. A kind word, asking how someone is doing, thanking someone, buying them a small gift, taking time to do something for them – these are all deposits into a relationship. The withdrawals are when you let someone down, or you forget something you committed to, or miscommunicate, or any number of things which lead to some hurt or disappointment.

When a withdrawal happens, and there's enough trust in the bank, things stay OK – saying sorry is making another deposit; there's grace in the system to rebuild trust.

The problems start when the account goes into the red: you're making more withdrawals than investments. There's just no trust left, and the relationship starts to go sour.

Do what you can to keep your relationships in the black. For, love covers a multitude of sins.[16]

I wanted to make lots of deposits into our relationship with our bishop. It meant we had a great relationship with him, our mother church, and those who supported us, through the discipline of writing every month.

This principle of making deposits and withdrawals from relationships is a really helpful metric to help gauge what might be going on when things become strained or difficult with a person or even a group of people. Have I made a significant withdrawal that has taken me into the red? Or have I made lots of little withdrawals without making many deposits?

Of course, it works the other way too – we have to learn to use the art of forgiveness when others make withdrawals from us. Modelling forgiveness is the way our team and church begin to see what it looks like. Painful as it may be, remember, it starts with you.

Relationships are the key way that the ripples will flow out of us into others as pioneers and planters. And those ripple effects are then multiplied out as others then grow in their call to see God's kingdom come. As we build good relationships with those who we are responsible for leading, those who we work alongside, and those to whom we are accountable, we begin to embody the love of Christ together and impact the community around us.

As we'll see, that's what incarnation looks like.

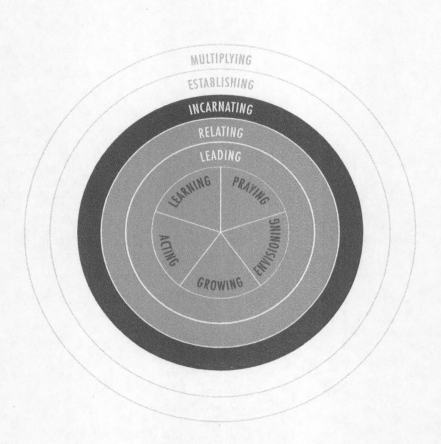

8

Incarnating

Chilli is one of my favourite meals. In these days of climate crisis, we try to eat more vegetable chilli, but every so often I love a good chilli con carne. Chilli with meat. That's what *carne* means: *meat*, or *flesh*.

Jesus was God-in-flesh: the In*carna*tion.

He was the fullness of God as human, and we as the body of Christ represent him in the world. Through our words and actions, we bring the good news 'in flesh' to people – we incarnate the good news of God's love to others. As one of my friends says, 'Your life is the only Bible some people will ever read.' We're the body of Christ: God in the flesh to those around us.

People, Not Projects

Incarnating is to do with how we embody the good news in the context where we're planting. It's about how we seek first his kingdom and strategically and practically live out God's love to those around us.

There are two things to keep in mind as we start living and serving within a community. First is that the greatest human need is to have a relationship with Father God through Jesus, empowered by the Holy Spirit. This is our goal: to see God's kingdom come on earth as in heaven, to see every knee bowing to Jesus as people come to a realisation of his love, forgiveness, and his rule and reign.

The second thing to remember is that incarnating the good news is about people, not projects. This is one of the great challenges of any organisation, which often initially start as a good work, focused on people. In order for the project to expand and have a wider impact, an organisation is formed.

But if you're not careful, you can start serving the project, not the people.

So we need to keep our focus on how we might introduce people to Jesus, and how we prioritise people not projects.

It is important to remember that incarnating doesn't mean just coming up with projects we like the idea of, but developing a strategy relevant to the context in which we find ourselves. Fresh Expressions, the movement which grew out of a response to the 2004 Church of England report 'Mission-Shaped Church, has demonstrated the power of contextualised mission.[1]

Most likely, as you've been relating to people and organisations around you, you'll have begun to pick up a flavour of the community where you're working, and some of the issues the people are facing.

What are their struggles? Their pain? Their immediate need? What does genuine mission look like here? What does genuine worship look like to these people?

What is good news to this community?

The answer to these questions always includes the message of the gospel of Jesus, but what actions might help demonstrate good news to these people, in this neighbourhood or this network?

In other words, the good news of Jesus remains the same regardless of context, but the *way* it is communicated must be sensitive to each community and person.[2]

As you consider the needs around you, and the opportunities you have to respond to them, you begin to develop your contextual strategy. It's a simple but hard thing to do: turn good ideas into sustained action.

And as you think about serving those in your context, you might need to think outside the box, to do things slightly differently to your normal expression of church. As Christians, it might feel like the obvious thing is to begin with a worship gathering. However, in our post-Christian culture, which has moved away from Christianity and its Christian heritage,[3] most people aren't looking for a new church. And if they are, they're probably Christians already.

So sometimes the right thing to do is to *not* launch with a public worship service, but begin with some outreach work, building relationships and seeing what opportunities flow from there.

Missional and Attractional

Balancing outreach with worship services is about getting the balance between being *missional* and *attractional*. These two words have been used a lot in the last two decades, meaning they likely have multiple definitions depending on who you're speaking to.

I'm referring to *missional* as a church defined primarily by its engagement with the community, where the quality of the worship gathering is secondary to the relationships already formed through mission. Relationships come first, and worship develops from there.

With *attractional*, I'm meaning a church that seeks to develop high-quality gatherings, a positive experience of welcome, hospitality and refreshments, engaging times of worship, social media presence ... you get the idea. Here, people are attracted to the 'brand' of your church.[4] A worship gathering comes first, and relationships with the community develop from there.

This doesn't necessarily mean that attractional-based church plants aren't missional and relational. And it doesn't necessarily mean that plants that start with a missional focus don't look to be attractional or eventually have gathered points of worship.

In conversations with pioneers and planters, I've found that many people see these two facets as polar opposites. I would argue it's probably more helpful to see them as two sides of the same coin. And they are both impacted by your context and calling.

At Glo Church, we planted onto a deprived social housing estate in Stockport, and our initial focus was building team and creating connections in the community. Once we moved in, we began to build relationships with the people in the community.

As already mentioned, we tried to open a coffee shop and considered opening a Free School. We also ran groups for teenage mums, helped support a community fun day, took assemblies and helped at the local primary school. Those kinds of things. We got to know people. It took a year before we launched public worship.

Once we did, it was simple, low-maintenance worship with music led by a guitar, and sometimes a cajón (box drum), amplified by a speaker designed for busking. We served refreshments in the middle of the meeting because we were renting a school hall and couldn't afford to pay for more time than we needed, and it took a while for the water to boil and to clear the cups away after. But it was great for our church, which was built on a strong sense of community. It was arguably a 'missional church'. Relationships came first; worship services developed out of that.

The challenge with Glo was to engage people beyond community into gathered worship.

When we planted Saint Philips Chapel Street, however, things were quite different. We were being launched as a church for the city, with a vision to plant other churches and draw people in from a wide area, which would also include some focus on our local context. As we were taking on public worship in a consecrated building, our first worship gathering was five days after we were commissioned. It was intentionally designed to be 'attractional' – high-quality worship with a band, great refreshments, good website and social media presence, relevant and engaging teaching – all excellent input on a Sunday, around which people could gather.

The challenge with Saint Philips was to engage people beyond gathered worship into community and mission.

I'd argue that any church needs to strike the balance between missional and attractional – they're not polar opposites after all. Everybody wants a worship experience to be engaging.[5] But a church which only exists for worship gatherings isn't fully incarnating the good news of Jesus; if we fail to engage with the community we're reaching out to, we're not really living as the body of Christ.

With, Not For

Incarnating the gospel means finding 'people of peace', as I described in the chapter on acting. We look for those who welcome us, listen to us and help us. So the first question shouldn't be, 'What can we do *to* this community?' but 'Who is God giving us in this community who we can work together *with*?'

Asking 'What can we do *together* for Jesus?' rather than 'What can we do *for* you?' is the key to finding people of peace in the community, and avoiding people joining your church because of what you can do for them (a consumer culture) as well as avoiding creating unhealthy dependencies. When Jesus sent out the Twelve and the seventy-two (in Matthew 10 and Luke 10), his strategy was for the disciples to go in weakness not strength, with questions not just answers, with humility not pride. We go in with two ears and only one mouth.

In this way, we begin to work *with* the community, not *for* the community. This is where the leaders need to be learners: finding out what God is doing, and joining in. It's important to avoid projects which are just our good ideas, but instead, as we're mining into the hearts and lives of the people we meet, to find the seam of gold where God is already at work.

Share the Good News

Evangelism. Evangelisation. Preaching the gospel. Sharing your faith.

Whatever you call it, it's absolutely essential to church planting.

Despite still being frequently quoted, it's almost certainly *not* true that St Francis of Assisi said, 'Preach the gospel at all times, and if necessary use words.'[6]

It's not enough to show the gospel through acts of service in the community. It's not enough to have the structures in place. It's not enough to have a great team, or a great venue, or some money behind you, or an awesome vision, if none of it includes sharing your faith with others.

Paul said to Timothy, 'do the work of an evangelist'.[7]

It doesn't matter if you feel gifted or not, the only way people who don't know about Jesus hear about him is if someone tells them.

As Paul writes to the Romans:

> How, then, can they call on the one they have not believed in? And how can they believe in the one of whom they have not heard? And how can they hear without someone preaching to them?[8]

As I mentioned in the chapter on learning, I'm not a natural evangelist. I want people to know about Jesus, but it's always felt a bit clumsy. So I started copying the way Lizzy, a natural evangelist, did it. Throwing Jesus into conversations with people who were not Christians; sharing a testimony of how God had helped or healed; offering to pray for them. It was a bit lumbering at first, but I got better.

Here's the thing: it's great to have evangelists on the team, but it's not just their job to tell other people about Jesus. It's their job to be a catalyst within your community to inspire others to tell people about Jesus. That's what Ephesians 4 is all about.

'Christ himself gave ... the evangelists ... to equip his people for works of service ...'[9]

Evangelism is everyone's job, including yours as the leader.[10] Allow the gifted evangelists in your community to encourage others to share their faith too. It's part of their gifting to be the fly in the ointment which provokes the church to remember, and keep front and centre, those who are not yet in the church.

John Wimber used to say, 'Keep the main thing the main thing', and the main thing we're doing in planting and pioneering is trying to give people who don't yet know Jesus the opportunity to be introduced to him.

That means the main thing is Jesus – not your church, your project, your good idea, your team, your vision. All those great things I just listed are some of the means by which we get to meet people and introduce them to Jesus.

Since we planted into central Manchester in Salford, we have run the Alpha course every term. It's a fantastic way of introducing people to the good news of Jesus, giving them a safe place to process their thoughts, hear other perspectives, and make a decision to follow Jesus for themselves.

But it's easy for the focus to get slightly off. When encouraging people to invite their friends to Alpha, we can sometimes make Alpha the focus, not Jesus. Do we want people talking about Alpha, or Jesus? Alpha is just a tool we can use to help people talk about Jesus; Alpha can't save people, only Jesus can. Alpha is not the point, Jesus is the point.

Are you a natural evangelist or perhaps a reluctant one? How can you grow in confidence in your ability to share the good news of Jesus? Who are the natural evangelists around you who can catalyse others into remembering the lost?

Offer Prayer

In my experience, the easiest way to introduce Jesus into a conversation – beyond talking about a project or our church – is to offer to pray for someone. When a person begins to tell you about their concerns, their needs or frustrations, their pain, struggles or suffering, we often can't do much more than point them to the best agency who might be skilled enough to help: the medical profession, a housing provider or council service.

But we can pray.

I've found people rarely turn down the offer of prayer. Most people don't feel like they can pray – either they feel like they're not good enough, or they wouldn't know how to begin. A Christian coming alongside them, putting words to their pain or suffering before the Lord, is a deeply encouraging experience for most people.

One of our neighbours owned a pub but was really concerned because it was in a challenging area of the city, and people were starting to deal drugs there. He knew the area had a reputation; he knew what was happening could damage the business and he could lose all of his investment. But he couldn't see a way out. Who would want to buy that off him? Along with all this, he was suffering with painful headaches, most likely brought on by stress.

There was nothing we could do other than offer some sympathy, and listen to his woes.

But we could pray.

He wasn't a Christian, and wasn't really interested in faith, but we offered to pray for him, and he accepted. We laid hands on him and asked for his headache to be healed in the name of Jesus, and for the Lord to help with his business.

He wasn't completely healed in that moment but did experience a significant amount of relief from his headache, and a deep sense of peace as we prayed.

The next day he went into work, someone walked into the pub and asked if it was up for sale, and made a cash offer there and then.

The next day!

He couldn't wait to tell us. We were so excited, all of us together, including his wife who had just become a Christian herself. We all agreed these answers to prayers were miraculous.

But here's the thing: he didn't make a decision to follow Jesus.

That's the way it worked with Jesus, too, right? Many were healed, but many chose not to follow him. Only one of the ten lepers came back to even say thank you for their healing. Others followed for a while, only to give up, as John's Gospel says: 'From this time many of his disciples turned back and no longer followed him.'[11]

But it didn't stop Jesus healing, or teaching, or loving people.

How often do you offer to pray for people, and do so, there in the moment? It's a good thing to try, and become natural at doing. Can you try it in the next couple of days? Can you model it to your team around you?

Organic *and* Organised

We incarnate the gospel to others as the body of Christ both in organic ways as individuals, but also as an organised activity. When we talk about the organised element of a church plant, it's about the established group or body of people. It means there's an organisation, a group, with a structure that people can identify and potentially choose to be connected with and part of.

In terms of *organic* incarnation, this encompasses everything we've already talked about regarding mission and evangelism, with each person on the team and in the church taking some responsibility for sharing their faith with their neighbours, friends, family, colleagues, classmates, gym buddies …

It's why, when we planted into a deprived estate in Stockport, we asked the team to move house to live there. We love the principles behind the Eden Network, established and run by The Message Trust: 'Eden sends and supports teams of urban missionaries to share the gospel, make disciples and rebuild communities.'[12]

The goal is to live alongside people, getting to know them, their dreams, hopes, fears and frustrations, and sharing Jesus with them in that context. Because you live in the same place, bump into people in the shops, on the street, in the pub … you're able to incarnate the gospel in multiple ways as you meet them, and seek to love and serve them. This might not always be on your own – Jesus sent the disciples in twos – but it's the informal embodiment of the good news in everyday life. For example, hosting a dinner party where some people are Christians and some are not – it's not organised by the church, it's just Christians sharing life with others.

But there's another way to incarnate the gospel too, which is *organised* – the church as a community, an organised group of people doing an organised event.

The very first event we put on when planting Glo Church was an Easter Sunday celebration in the local park. We didn't have a building, so we blew up some balloons, put on some music, and organised some party games for the kids. We also shared some testimonies and a reflection about Easter, and one of our guys who was in a band did some rapping. Around sixty people turned up that day to an event we'd organised as a community – one person couldn't have pulled it off on their own, but together we could make an impact.

We also regularly ran 'serve days' in the community, where we would gather together, put on our church T-shirts, and go out to be a blessing – by litter picking, doing free car washes, clearing people's back gardens etc.

One particular time we noticed a pile of bin bags in the back garden of one of the families we knew. The mum didn't have a car, and with eight children, produced far more waste than her bin could take every week. Feeling overwhelmed, she started to put them outside the back door, but they began to gather and fester. We took over eighty full bin bags to the tip when we cleared her garden. Yes, there were used nappies. And yes, some of the bin bags split open and spilled everywhere.

Gross.

But it was also an amazing way of demonstrating the love of Jesus. We tried to encourage her to help in the clear up, and to get in touch with the council to provide another bin so it wouldn't happen again.

In Salford, Lizzy launched 'Bags of Hope' – ten items in a cloth bag for asylum seekers, vulnerable women, the homeless and struggling local families. It's a brilliant project that both individuals and institutions can get involved with. Individuals pick up an empty bag with a shopping list attached to it, with items appropriate for the intended recipient. They buy those ten items, write a note on the tag, and bring it back to the church. We then drop the bags off to various charities we're connected with in the city centre.

There was one guy in our church who got his whole department at work to take it on as their sponsored charity – dozens of people who were not part of the church took a bag, filled it, and were able to be a blessing to others; the church making the most of organic relationships to reach out as an organisation.

Because of this work, some of the most vulnerable in our community have been blessed with a bag full of toiletries, underwear, and other items to regain a little dignity.

One woman wrote to us to say that getting a Bag of Hope was the start of her journey of recovery. It provided the small spark she needed to begin to rebuild her life.

I'm not suggesting that all those people who filled a Bag of Hope became Christians, or that everyone who receives one turns to faith. But they provide an amazing opportunity to have the conversation about Jesus with people.

We can do that through our informal, organic interactions *and* our church's organised interactions.

It's using every opportunity to introduce Jesus into our relationship with people. Not just introducing the church, or the project, but using those things to talk about Jesus.

Paul's famous speech at the Areopagus[13] is a reminder to all of us pioneers and planters that although the basic facts of the gospel do not change, the way we communicate it can vary from context to context. Paul's strategy before arriving in Athens was to go into the synagogue and preach about the Messiah. This would convince some, but not everyone. A church was planted with those who were convinced, Paul raised up leaders, and then moved on, often due to persecution from those who were not convinced.

In Athens, however, Paul takes a different strategy. He was there for his own safety, as the unconvinced had started to stir ill feeling towards him in Berea, where he had been staying. So he wasn't in Athens to church plant like normal; he was there for his own wellbeing.

Paul being Paul, however, couldn't help but share the gospel. He did his normal thing of going to the synagogue, but also threw himself into the philosophical debating that went on in the city. (I love Luke's description of Athens: 'All the Athenians and the foreigners who lived there spent their time doing nothing but talking about and listening to the latest ideas.'[14] I always get the sense Luke wasn't impressed!)

When Paul starts to share the gospel, he uses a completely different strategy to engage those who had no idea of the old covenant. He uses their own poets and philosophers to build his case. He's read the culture, understood the culture, and uses the culture to present the good news of Jesus.

This is contextualisation at its finest, and we can learn a lot from Paul. Here he is, as an individual, incarnating the good news of Jesus in an *organic* way to a group of people who were unfamiliar with the Jewish story of redemption and were not awaiting the Messiah.

Earlier in Acts, however, we see the church as an *organisation* – as a group of people – incarnating the gospel, through providing food to the poor: cooking the food, setting out tables and serving it out to the widows among them. The church being a blessing. Doing more than one person could do on their own.

Organised mission is mission together, as community – you're representing in your individual actions something bigger than yourself, the group to which you belong. It's the church community having an impact in the wider community.

If you're helping a colleague, or having neighbours around for Christmas drinks, or bringing in their bins, or offering to pray for a friend who doesn't know Jesus and is going through a hard time – then it's organic incarnation. If it's a church litter pick, Alpha course, food bank or Christmas lunch, then it's organised incarnation.

The point is, we need both. One feeds the other. People are more likely to trust the church as an organisation if they personally know a Christian who loves and serves them and others.

Like your teachers always said, when you wear the uniform, you represent the school, and your actions reflect upon the school.

Once people know we are Christians, the uniform never comes off. Christian means 'little Christs' – in many ways we *are* Jesus to them. Remember, we might be the only Bible they ever read.

How can you incarnate the gospel individually where you are? What ways can you do things together as a group to share the good news of Jesus? Have you taken the time to research the demographics of those you are reaching to identify their needs and concerns? Can you connect with local charities to see how you might help with what's already going on?

Contextual Worship

If the principle of contextualisation is true for our mission, then I would argue it must also be true for our worship. Mark Sayers has made an excellent case against 'relevant' church,[15] but the church has always tended towards one of two extremes:

separatism – being so distinct to the point of unusual and strange; or
syncretism – so similar to the culture it's hard to tell it's the church.

Separatism is where churches behave in such a way that it separates those 'outside' of the church from those 'inside'. It requires a huge cultural leap for someone who has never been part of church before. Some monasteries functioned like this – trying to escape the world and choosing not to engage with it. The Amish might act as a more extreme modern example, but separatism is also taking place in those churches that resist singing more up-to-date songs or insist on sticking with sixteenth-century language.

But we can be guilty of this too, for example when we don't explain what we're doing in church and why. If someone begins to prophesy or speak in tongues, and we assume everyone knows what's happening, we're building a culture that's separate to those outside the church. Overusing religious language also demarcates us against an 'outsider'. Culture gets built – either on purpose or by accident. But it does get built. Separatism at its worst makes an onlooker think, 'I can't connect with this. It's completely irrelevant to me and my life.'

Syncretism is at the opposite end of the scale; where a church looks so like the surrounding culture there's not much to distinguish it. The senior pastor of one of the churches I served in when we lived in the US admitted that for a season before we came they stopped mentioning Jesus in their Sunday gatherings because they didn't want to offend people. They had come out of the seeker church model and taken things to quite an extreme. They gave positive messages on a Sunday in the hope that people might wonder why and come along midweek to hear about Jesus. Christian worship had become presentation of some nice positive thoughts rather than participation in a communal act of honouring Jesus.

That's how syncretism works – it dilutes the gospel to the point that it doesn't really mean anything anymore.

I'd argue that worship in our church community needs to find the middle ground between syncretism and separatism. We don't reduce the gospel to look so similar to the culture around it that it is no different at all; but we also don't keep our worship so culturally distinct that nobody can understand what is going on. We proclaim it afresh in our generation.

As we seek to embody the good news of Jesus, in word and deed, as individuals and as a community, we incarnate the body of Christ to those around us. Often, as the organisation, this may well develop into regular things we do – a toddler group, a foodbank, a job club, midweek groups, gathered worship – which need organising, sustaining and supporting.

Which takes us on to our next step: establishing.

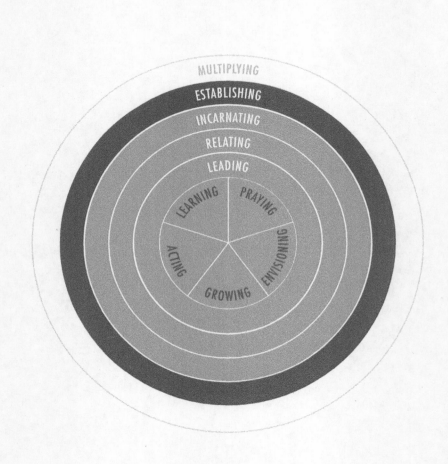

9

Establishing

David J. Bosch in *Transforming Mission* wrote, 'any social organization, in order to persist, must have boundaries, must maintain structural stability as well as flexibility, and must create a unique culture'.[1]

Any community has to have a shape – a rhythm. Groups develop structures, governance and traditions, and it's the pioneer's job to work out how best to create a framework around which the newly formed community of faith can continue to grow, become sustainable and eventually multiply.

The structure you need when you're a small planting team is quite different to the structure required once the church has grown. When you're a small team, you're able to spend lots of time together, sharing the vision, dreaming together, and processing what's going on. Once things grow, and the team have areas of responsibility, along with their own teams to lead, there are more demands on everyone's time, and things have to work differently.

Paul's work in Ephesus gives us some insight into the establishing phase.

His first visit to the city was when he was passing through on the way to Jerusalem.[2] He preached in the synagogue one Sabbath and was asked to stay on, but instead went on his way. Priscilla and Aquila, who had helped Paul previously in Corinth, stayed in Ephesus. It seems they carried on building relationships and incarnating the gospel, leading people towards Jesus, because by the time Paul came back, there were twelve guys who believed in Jesus and who then received the baptism of the Spirit.[3]

A split within the synagogue ensued, and Paul then spent the next two years having 'discussions daily in the lecture hall of Tyrannus'.[4]

Eventually things started kicking off in Ephesus against Paul's teaching, and a riot began (ever caused a riot because of your mission?!). Paul left, and went back to visit churches he had planted in Macedonia, where he 'travelled through that area, speaking many words of encouragement to the people'.[5]

However, a few months later he was travelling back past Ephesus and met the elders of the Ephesian church in Miletus. He encouraged them, 'Keep watch over yourselves and all the flock of which the Holy Spirit has made you overseers. Be shepherds of the church of God, which he bought with his own blood.'[6]

Paul's focus in Ephesus moved from the initial work of leading, relating and incarnating to *establishing* the work of God.

Timothy became the leader of the church in Ephesus, and the letter of 1 Timothy was written by Paul to help Timothy in the work of establishing the church there. It has lessons on teaching and preaching, corporate worship, leadership development, as well as personal encouragement and wisdom from an older leader to a younger one.

Everywhere Paul went on mission, he sought to raise up leaders and pass on the leadership of the community to them. His concern was for those who had responded to Jesus to be pastored well, and for the mission of God to continue to reach those who didn't yet know Jesus.

He sought to establish the work the Holy Spirit had begun by finding trustworthy people who could become good leaders and continue the work of the church, both in pastoral care and mission outreach once he had gone.

The same is true for us today. The aim is to build something that will last, not just celebrate some short-term success which dies soon after we leave.

The question is, how?

Structured for Growth

A while back, Lizzy and I bought some new plants for our garden. We're not great gardeners by any means, but we love nature and like the idea of being surrounded by healthy plants and greenery in what a friend calls our 'yarden': our little walled garden in the city. We wanted some climbing plants up the east-facing wall, so we researched which ones would be best, and bought the plants.

The plants came with little stakes to support them as they grew. Because they wouldn't stick to the wall themselves, I had to put a trellis on the wall to support them as they got bigger. Honestly, from my inexperienced-gardener perspective, it looked a bit silly for a couple of months: these tiny plants sticking out of the ground, and a big, empty trellis on the wall above them.

Then they started to grow.

And wow, did they grow.

By the end of the summer, the trellis was covered.

It was wonderful for us – we had these beautiful plants climbing our wall, giving us the greenery we'd hoped for. But if they hadn't had the trellis, all that growth would have spilled across the floor. It wouldn't have looked beautiful, but messy. The plants wouldn't have been healthy, and we'd have wasted all the energy the plant put into growing.

The structures we try to establish are like the trellis to support the plant. Those structures aren't the life of the church, but they help to support it, and without them, life and growth won't be sustainable.

Settling Down

Initially, church planting is like putting a tiny seed into a propagator and creating an environment where it can sprout. It's weak and vulnerable. You may be a very small team, researching the needs within the area, getting to know the demographic or geographic situation as it stands, starting something from scratch.

Then you take the little sprouting seed out of the propagator into a slightly larger pot, to help continue the growth. It still needs care and attention, but it is no longer quite as vulnerable. This is the stage when your planting team are getting things up and running, beginning to grow, putting in the essentials to help things continue and develop.

Eventually, you put the seedling into the ground so that it can grow and flourish. The establishing stage is about settling down and making the whole thing functional.

The leader has to work to embed the five characteristics – praying, envisioning, growing, acting and learning – into the community, and implement practices and rhythms to help establish these values at the heart of everything, making the whole thing safe and healthy for growth.

This settling stage is the longer, slower work of establishing what has been pioneered so that it can continue in the long run, helping people feel connected in community, creating effective structures and rhythms to sustain the shared life together. It's the marathon, not the sprint.

We need each other, and for each member of the team to play to their strengths in every stage, and this is as true in the establishing phase as in any other. Each stage allows different natural giftings to flourish, as author Nathan Brewer notes:

> The functions of the fivefold provide mobility and stability. Generally speaking, apostles and prophets are pioneering and *mobile*, advancing the kingdom of God to new places, whereas evangelists, shepherds, and teachers stay longer in one place and mature the existing work, with the shepherds and teachers

especially providing *stability* in relationships and in God's Word. (Evangelists are, of course, also mobile as they go out to share the gospel. However, they tend to bring people back to an established work, rather than starting a new one). ... these two groups [can be] classified as the 'Start and Go' team (apostles and prophets), and the 'Stay and Grow' team (evangelists, shepherds, and teachers). One 'team' is not better than the other; both are needed for healthy kingdom growth.[7]

In the first three stages of leading, relating and incarnating, the 'Start and Go' team thrive, but in the establishing stage, the 'Stay and Grow' team come into their own. The pastors and teachers are more naturally gifted at building on the work that has been pioneered by the 'Start and Go' team. Establishing provides the structure, the stability, the repeating patterns – the 'norm' – to allow the wider church to flourish and grow.

As the initial planting team began to grow at Saint Philips Chapel Street, we were able to support some people pastorally, but we were aware of our limitations. We couldn't look after everyone. So we established 'Connect Groups' where people could connect (get it?) in a small group environment with each other, with God, and with the mission to see others come to faith. These small groups are our primary pastoral structure, so it's down to us to help the Connect Group leaders do their job as well as they can, by giving them time, training and vision.

As we saw in the learning and leading chapters, part of delegating well involves discerning where people are in their own leadership development.

If someone in your team is *unconsciously incompetent*, that determines how much responsibility and authority you give them. It would be unsafe for them, and for the people in the church, if they took on too much.

If someone is struggling in their confidence as they're becoming *consciously incompetent*, you'll need to spend time with them to remind them what they're doing and why, give lots of grace as they learn and offer help when needed.

Similarly, as someone becomes *consciously competent*, you'll become more confident in releasing tasks to them.

Once a team member is *unconsciously competent*, you'll be more than happy to let them get on with things.

So leaders need to use different leadership skills for different people in their varying stages of development.

In *When to Walk Away*, author and speaker Gary Thomas writes that as Christian leaders the best thing we can do is 'exactly what 2 Timothy 2:2 and Matthew 6:33 call you to do'[8] – focus on investing in reliable people, and seeking first God's kingdom.

This is how you develop a leadership pipeline: raising up others to help establish, and eventually multiply, the work. As we build team, we discover people who are trustworthy and reliable, and we pour ourselves into them. The goal is to develop a team that functions with *low control* but *high accountability*.

At Saint Philips, we wanted to recruit someone to lead our kids work who, at a minimum, was already functioning as consciously competent. We shared the vision with Rick Otto and his wife, Claire, who sensed the call to join us and become part of the team. We were thrilled to welcome them and love having Rick as our kids and youth worker. He's head of children's work within New Wine, so he's trusted by a whole bunch of people beyond just us to lead excellent, inspiring kids work.

Rick threw himself into everything, and began to build a kids ministry, which continued to grow as church members formed relationships and incarnated the gospel with those in their community. At the time of writing, Rick currently has the challenge of not having enough space for the kids who come on a Sunday morning and so is focusing on the work of establishing the ministry: training leaders, delegating, creating the system, structures and repeating patterns to help create meaningful community for the kids at our church.

He's accountable to us, but we don't control how he does things. At least, that's the plan. Sometimes we get it wrong: sometimes we might express a thought or conviction too strongly, and come across as controlling. Sometimes we'll assume everything's going fine and neglect to bring effective accountability.

The aim is for both the team leader and the team member to be clear on the goals they are going after, and reach towards them together. The leader's role in this is to offer support and challenge to help the team member do all they can to achieve those objectives.

This requires trust and love, which must be nurtured over time, through both time in the team together, and time one-to-one.

Establishing Structure

There are many questions you'll need to consider as you move into the establishing phase of your plant. When do you meet? What do you do? What sets you apart from other communities similar to you? How is the life of the community funded? How does a newcomer enter the community? Is someone a part of the church if they come to the church gatherings but are not yet a believer in Jesus? In what way? What role do the sacraments play? How does the community govern itself, and how does it relate to the wider body of Christ?

These go alongside questions of leadership. Who will lead what? Who is taking responsibility for different aspects? How do you develop structures that release people into their God-given gifting?

And how do you do all of this while continuing to have relationships with people coming to faith, walking a pathway of discipleship with them?

These are massive questions. Some of them will be defined by the denomination out of which you're planting. Some of them will be forced upon you by circumstances. But others you will have to work out in your context.

When we planted in Stockport, I was a paid staff member of the mother church in a different town. I led worship or preached on the Sunday mornings and evenings at the mother church, and so our planting team met on Sunday afternoons. As we got to know the people where we were planting, it turned out Sunday afternoon was a pretty good time to gather for worship, so the practice stuck.

Our governance and finances were covered by the mother church. We didn't have a building, so we just met in venues we could find and afford. We had a few small groups, but throughout our time there we never grew beyond about sixty people, so it was a community where everyone knew everyone else.

Moving to Salford to plant into a building which already had an existing congregation of around fifteen older people was quite a different experience, with different questions. There was already Sunday worship – so when would the new planting congregation meet? There was a church council, so governance was already established. There was a £10 million, iconic Georgian building to maintain. We grew to 250 people within three years, so nobody could possibly know everybody.

Our contexts asked different questions of us; some of which were easy to resolve, others took more time. Some we're still working through.

The establishing phase requires all five of the characteristics. Through *prayer* and *vision* you find some kind of idea of what you're aiming for. You keep *growing* through it all as you take *action* by trying different ideas, and you continue to *learn* more about the context, your team, and how best to lead.

Getting out and meeting people, finding ways to tell them about Jesus, is a very different thing to organising the finances of a community. Pulling together a meaningful time for the community to gather and worship is not the same as creating the structures and rhythms that will help sustain the community.

There will be some skills you're naturally good at, and some you will need to learn, or ask other people to take on. Leaders don't have to do everything, but they do have to make sure everything gets done.

Establishing Community

As we begin to nurture a community life, it's helpful to understand the various ways people connect with one another and find a sense of community, so that we can establish the best patterns and practices for common life.

In his book, *The Search to Belong*, Joseph Myers suggests that humans need four groups of various sizes and varying depth of relationship to gain a sense of belonging.[9] He takes this principle from sociology and applies it to the church, using the terms *intimate, personal, social* and *public.*

The *intimate* relationships are those you have with only one or two other people. They know pretty much everything there is to know about you, and it's mutual. This is the person with whom you can be completely honest and they will still love you. It's the context God gives us to deal with our deepest shame. Sometimes a therapist might play this role. (In this case the relationship isn't mutual, but the point is the same: it's someone with whom we can be completely honest.) In the process, we learn about ourselves and find God's grace. Intimate relationships are a place to 'confess your sins to each other and pray for each other so that you may be healed'.[10]

Similarly, you may get to know someone who is not a Christian and have many deep, significant conversations where you help them, on a one-to-one basis, wrestle with some of the questions they have on their journey of faith.

Not all relationships can be that intense, though.

We'd all be exhausted.

Yet as leaders it's key to encourage these closer, more intimate relationships, to help people belong and grow effectively in their life of faith.

During the Covid-19 lockdown, I was speaking to our student leaders who were concerned for many of our university students. We put in place a plan to create prayer triplets – a more intimate space than a small group, where three students of the same gender could share what's going on for them and pray for each other. An intimate space to share, support and grow. We're now encouraging all of our church to have an accountability partner or spiritual companion with whom we can walk our journey of faith.

How might you provide a structure for people to grow in an intimate Christian friendship?

The next size grouping that gives us a sense of community is the *personal*: the six to ten people who know you really well.

This might be your immediate family, or in a church context, it's your small group: the people you see regularly who know many of the things going on in your life.

These small groups offer a place for people to grow in their character and relationship with God, and to learn to use their own gifts in ministry with one another; they provide a place for new leaders to be identified and released; and they model in the small what we want to see happening in the big – raising up leaders and planting new groups.

Christian Schwarz, in his groundbreaking classic *Natural Church Development*, uses the terminology of 'holistic small groups' which 'go beyond just discussing Bible passages to applying its message to daily life. In these groups, members are able to bring those issues and questions that are of immediate personal concern.'[11] After taking 4.2 million surveys across the world, small groups made it into his top eight essential qualities to help support church growth.

Through the years, we've had a number of people join our small group a long time before they ever thought of coming to church. For these people, a small gathering where they could share life with a few people felt like the safest place for them to begin their faith journey, or rebuild trust with 'the church'. Some people find smaller groups more intimidating, and prefer the relative anonymity of a larger group, but for others, small groups are a great way to welcome people into the family of God.

So what do small groups look like in your context? How will you create a structure of support and challenge for the leaders of these groups?

The *social* sphere recognises that humans have a limit to the number of people they can know in any meaningful way, and this tops out at around seventy people. Some have capacity for more, and some for less, but seventy seems to be around the average.

In a church context, this social sphere is most akin to a congregation; some larger churches break down into missional communities of around this size too. Seventy people means most people can know and recognise each other. We know a little bit about everyone in our social sphere – some more, some less – but we notice when there's someone new. And this can present a challenge: it's quite intimidating for someone to just walk into a church without knowing anyone. You know you're going to be noticed.

One of the big challenges for church leaders is to encourage people to break out of their normal human instincts to sit in the same place each week, and catch up with just the people we know. Lizzy and I work hard to ensure the people we speak to on a Sunday are the leaders and the newcomers. We want our church culture to be one where all our people notice and welcome newcomers. We need to talk to the leaders, so the gathering can go as planned, but we also try to make a beeline for the newcomers, so that we can welcome them.

We try to have a number of social events as a church throughout the year, which allow people to get to know one another beyond the context of a worship gathering, and for those on the fringe to connect more fully.

How can you ensure people connect well at a social level, in a way that welcomes the newcomer and gives time to the people we know well?

Finally, there's the *public* sphere.

This sphere includes the courier who regularly drops something off at your door – you don't really know anything about them, but you recognise them. Or the checkout assistant at your local shop. We might remember their face; but we would never say we *know* them. In church, this will likely include the fringe people who may not even have faith but would come to a social gathering. For those in larger churches, it's the people who worship at different services, or the people we might recognise who sit in very different places to us – we don't know their names, but we get a sense of belonging just because we are both in the same place and have seen each other around.

Some people find this anonymity the safest place to be, and enjoy being able to sit at the back of church, listening, reflecting, and arriving late and leaving early as they begin to slowly trust the environment and the people before wanting to build any deeper connections.

This anonymity can also create a deep sense of loneliness when we don't have the other three spheres; so, someone who has recently moved to a new city will feel that everybody is in the public sphere. Work colleagues or continuing a hobby will quickly provide the social sphere, and some from that may develop into the personal sphere. In our mobile culture, often the personal and intimate spheres contain people who don't live near us in our new context, but are friends from back home or uni or the place we used to live.

What might the public sphere look like in your context? How could you encourage your people to connect to the those on the fringes, beyond the people they know well?

When we look at the life of Jesus, we can observe him relating to others in all these spheres. He had Peter, James and John as his closest friends, with John as his 'intimate' friend. Then he had the Twelve – the personal sphere. He would teach the Twelve things that others wouldn't get to hear; he would give them access to his life more than others; there was a greater sense of trust; and they were the first to be sent out on mission by Jesus.[12] Then there were the seventy-two – the social sphere – also sent out by Jesus on mission.[13] They obviously shared Jesus' vision and heart for mission and were trusted by him.[14] And he also engaged in the public sphere, with the crowds who listened to and followed him.

I recently had coffee with a guy who was thinking of joining our church, longing for a sense of community with other young adults who are trying to follow Jesus. He'd been coming along to our Sunday worship but not feeling connected to people. I talked through these four places of belonging, and he realised he was looking for closer, more *personal* connection in the place of *social* connection – a tough ask. So I encouraged him to go along to a Connect Group, a small group, and see if there might be the potential for that deeper sense of belonging there.

People can access church community through all of these spheres, and so we need to build them into our structures to help people belong.

How can you establish structures that help connect people in all four spaces? What can you do to encourage people to establish intimate spiritual companions? How can you raise up more small group leaders and encourage people to join them? Where are the places of social connection beyond Sundays? And how can you create public gatherings that both serve your people and welcome the outsider?

Missional *and* Pastoral

A huge challenge within the establishing stage is to continue keeping the focus on why you planted in the first place: to see those who don't yet know Jesus come to faith in him.

Planting starts with a small, passionate group of people who love Jesus and are committed to the vision of seeing God's kingdom come through the establishment of a new missional and worshipping community.

Each of those people carry with them challenges and issues they will face. And they will be looking to you as the leader to help pastor them through it, which will be a valid demand on your time. As will maintaining all the relationships established in steps two (relating) and three (incarnating). And all the paperwork and meetings that come with good governance. And planning worship. And sustaining your own prayer life. And family. And so it goes on.

There's a lot to do. It's why team is so important; there's no way you can do all this alone.

And it can be easy to lose the missional edge, simply by virtue of doing a really great job of looking after the people you already have.

So your structures have to embrace and enable both *pastoral* work and *missional* work.

This means giving people time to understand the missional DNA, to hear the heart of the leader and of the church, and to catch the vision – that we planted for the sake of others. This requires repeating the vision; reminding people why you're doing what you're doing; sowing the idea that you will plant another church in the future; telling the stories of those coming to faith; and giving airtime to individuals who have been engaging with others missionally, as well as those who have responded to Jesus because of that mission.

This is one reason why Alpha and other such courses are so helpful in serving outreach: the Alpha team creates a group within the church committed to focused mission over a period of time. As they share stories with the wider church of people coming to faith and being transformed by Jesus, it sows seeds of faith and expectation that God is on the move.

Churches need pastoral structures – it's one reason why small groups are so important – but they also need missional structures where everyone is encouraged to get involved in multiplying their faith into other people.

This is easier said than done. There may be times when you feel more attention needs to be paid to the pastoral work. Then at other times, the focus is the missional imperative. But it's our job as leaders to establish rhythms and patterns to help serve both the pastoral needs of our community and the missional needs of our context.

We're more likely to be naturally focused on one than another. Lizzy and I are more focused on the growing edge of the church. We do this bit naturally. It takes more effort for us to focus on the pastoral stuff within church. This relates back to why we need each of the fivefold ministries. There are people in our church who are natural pastors, and though it's never our intention, they can sometimes feel disempowered by our focus on the mission. So establishing leaders for pastoral needs and leaders for missional work is vital, but there will always be a tension.

The result of not keeping mission in sight is that we lose our *raison d'être*. Perhaps you can think of some churches that are getting smaller over time because they forgot to sustain their missional edge. Pastoral work is key, but if we become overwhelmed by the pastoral, and forget the missional work of passing on our faith, it's simple maths that our church will eventually die.

What has been your experience of balancing missional and pastoral work? Where have you seen it done well? What is the result if there is a focus on just one, instead of both?

Leadership *and* Governance

Any initiative that lasts any length of time turns into an institution. There's no way we can stop this most human of processes – taking an idea someone had, and trying to build on it, or extend it, or multiply it, means it will go beyond just one person doing something, to others replicating it.

It's a good thing. It means others get it. It means it can last beyond me and you.

There's nothing wrong with institutions. There is, however, something wrong with institutionalisation: becoming caught up with sustaining the institution, so that you're serving *it*, rather than serving *others*, the very thing the institution was established to do. Institutionalisation means being unable to think outside the box of the institution.[15]

To help your church plant or pioneering work remain effective, you need to have both *leadership* (people alongside you helping to deliver the vision and mission of the church), and *governance* (people alongside you, keeping you accountable and ensuring you're doing what you're meant to be doing).

It's important to understand the balance between leadership and governance. Many pioneers resist the idea of governance and institution, thinking that these things tie them down, restricting them from doing the things they want to do.

There is some truth in this – but what we might sometimes view as restriction can also be viewed as focus.

Poor governance means that every idea the pioneer has needs to go through systems and processes, getting majority approval, slowing things down, so that the leaders are unable to respond quickly to anything. There is a lack of trust, and a lack of freedom. Good governance, however, creates both trust and freedom; it supports the leadership by helping them make sure they are doing what they say they are going to do, and by creating and sustaining healthy processes and systems to maintain the good work.

In the New Testament, there is reference to overseers, presbyters and deacons – different people taking on different roles within the church to allow the work of the Holy Spirit to flourish. And in the council of Jerusalem, detailed in Acts 15, we get a little glimpse into how governance worked: a group of people trying to disagree well, and discern God's word in the midst of their disagreement.[16]

At Glo Church, we didn't really have to worry too much about governance, as we were covered by the PCC (church council) of our mother church. Moving to Saint Philips Chapel Street was a challenge because we inherited a small congregation who already had a PCC, so we needed to work out how pioneering and planting worked alongside and in partnership with the governance structures already established.

I'm grateful to a friend's father-in-law who helped me think through good governance. He's been the head of both a national company and an international charity and has sat on multiple boards, so he knows a thing or two about governance. He suggests that the leaders are responsible for the vision and direction of the church, whereas the trustees of the church provide governance by offering high-level oversight and accountability over four things:

1. Strategy (vision)
2. Operating plan (budget)

3. Assets (building etc)
4. Support (looking after the team)

Mutual respect is best fostered between governance and leadership when the leadership trust the governance to offer high-level oversight and accountability, and when the governance resist getting bogged down in the details and trust the leadership to effectively implement the work.

This is best achieved by leadership communicating effectively on a regular basis, so that governance understands the challenges and opportunities the leadership faces. Effective governance considers recommendations put forward by the leadership, and agrees a course of action, which is then implemented by the leadership. When done well, the role of governance should be to help sharpen the plans of the leadership, and to ensure they are more of a blessing to the leadership than a burden.

When it comes to communication between leadership and governance, I've learned that more is better than less; it's what helps trust flow. However, this isn't instinctive for me (I'm a Gen-Xer – we're typically suspicious of institutions!), so I'm continuing to learn and grow to help make leadership and governance work better together.

Where have you seen leadership and governance done well? What made it successful? How are you going to communicate with those who carry the legal and financial responsibilities for the work? How can you develop relationships with them so you all experience it as a blessing rather than a burden?

The primary goal of establishing the work which has been initiated is ensuring its sustainability. To do this you will need help – people who are good with money; people who can establish you as a charity, or follow up with paperwork in other ways; people who are good with policies and procedures ... Not many pioneers get very excited about this stuff, but it's all really important.

Only once you've established something healthy, can you then go on to *plant* something healthy.

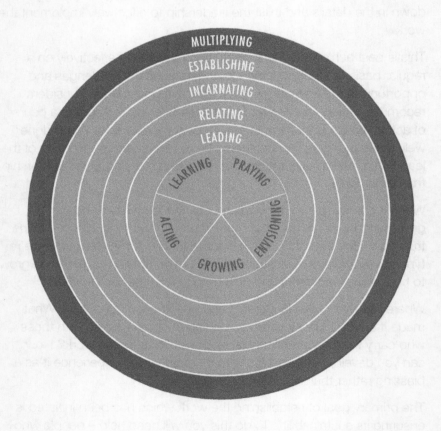

10

Multiplying

Jesus said he wanted us to be fruitful.

I don't know about you, but I hear the parable of the sower, and I long to be one who is fruitful to the point of multiplying thirty, sixty or one hundred times.[1] Following the example of Jesus, this means first investing in others and releasing people.

Ric Thorpe, Bishop of Islington, who has helped encourage many church plants within the Church of England, asserts that the Great Commission is actually a church-planting strategy. We are commissioned with authority from Jesus to go and make disciples – share with others what we have learned, so that they can do the same. We're instructed to baptise them, and teach them: exactly the things a church does. Jesus is calling us to create new communities, empowered by the Holy Spirit, which multiply the life that is in you and me.

It's the Holy Spirit who leads us, guides us, empowers us. It's the Holy Spirit who helps make us fruitful. John 15, the amazing passage about bearing kingdom fruit, is sandwiched between chapters 14 and 16, both of which describe the person and work of the Holy Spirit. We can't do this without him. What he pours *into* us, he longs to pour into others *through* us.

I love our three kids dearly. At the moment, they are all teenagers, a stage of life Lizzy and I are loving. But it's a very different stage of life to when they were toddlers.

We don't read picture books before bed anymore.

We don't help with bath time anymore. (That would be weird.)

We don't take them to school anymore, make their lunch anymore, go to play parks anymore …

Or find babysitters anymore. (We really like this one.)

We have to choose to make time to be with our kids now, because they are teenagers and don't need us in the same way they did when they were toddlers. And, in a few months, they will start to leave home.

That's the point.

They're *meant* to leave home. They're not meant to stick around, dependent on us, without the skills to navigate life.

Us parents have eighteen years to get these amazing bundles of joy ready to take on the world as responsible adults. We don't do that by clinging on to them.

But the idea of letting them go is so, so hard.

A parental relationship with a child becomes skewed when a parent derives their own sense of worth or value through their child. If a parent *needs* their child, they will do all sorts of things to try to keep them dependent.

In the same way, if we as leaders are going to see multiplication, we need to be secure enough to encourage it to happen.

Jackie Pullinger has said that the statement 'I want to make a difference' is self-centred – it's about *you*. It's about how much *you* can see happen, how much *you* can do, how much *you* will be remembered in history.

Ouch.

Instead, she argued we should be saying, 'I want to make disciples.' Making disciples is about giving away, selflessly investing into others, not to see what *you* can do, but to see what *others* can do.

Multiplying is about having a kingdom vision that goes way beyond your work, your ministry, your church. It's about preferring others in love – wanting the best for them and cheering them on as they capture a vision for what could be. It means being selfless – dying to self, to your dreams for how other people might serve *your* vision, dying to *your* way of doing it.

None of this comes naturally to us – but it is the gospel of Jesus.

Multiplying involves seeing people step out in faith to respond to God's call, but it can also mean loss. The loss of good people in the sending group, the loss of relationship on both sides, the loss of financial support as people move on. But these things also create an opportunity for others to step up – perhaps others we hadn't considered before because we hadn't yet needed them.

Raising Up, Sending Out

The research that came out of our pioneer and planter days suggests that multiplication happens in two different ways.

The first is that new people are released into leadership where you already are. The more people you have in your community viewing themselves as leaders, taking responsibility, owning the vision and doing what they can to seek first God's kingdom, the bigger impact the church will have for those who don't yet know Jesus.

One guy in our church recently came to faith on Alpha, then began to worship with us. He's passionate about helping young people, so has gone through the process of joining our youth team as a helper. In time, the prayer, hope and intention is that he becomes someone who can be a youth leader.

Another woman came to know Jesus after a friend at her gym invited her to church. Now she's serving on the team that works with vulnerable women.

Two people who have moved from being outside God's kingdom into being a fruitful part of kingdom work. Perhaps in time they will have a vision of their own, then develop and lead a new ministry within the church.

That's one way of multiplying.

How can you intentionally raise up other leaders to release both responsibility and authority to others within your context? What roles can you delegate as you lead and invest in people, so that they can grow and develop, and become leaders in their own right?

The second way to multiply is to send people out to plant a new church or pioneering work.

While we were at Glo, there were a number of people who joined us for a season and then sensed God call them on to something else. Each time the conversation with those individuals was hard, because these were good people who were serving on teams and making a real difference in people's lives through our church plant. But they sensed God calling them onwards.

At that point we had a choice: do we beg them to stay and make them feel guilty enough so they don't leave? Do we get the hump and tell them just to go, without getting the chance to say goodbye? Or do we try to get behind their kingdom vision, pray for and commission them publicly and celebrate what God is doing?

Of course, the last one is the right thing – but it's also the hardest.

These two ways of multiplying have a different impact on the current context. I would suggest a truly growing, healthy church would encourage both types of multiplication.

The dream is for new believers to become passionate followers of Jesus, taking on the five characteristics themselves, and stepping out to have a ripple effect on others. It can take some time, and is not without its challenges, but this surely has to be our vision:

To make disciples who make disciples.

To plant churches that plant churches means thinking about multiplication from the very beginning. So, as you plant a new church, you already have multiplication in mind.

That means considering who you can begin to take on a leadership pipeline, not just for the fruitfulness of your own church, but for an individual's development as a leader in God's kingdom.

Wisdom from Donors

Although Lizzy and I have raised up people into leadership, and sent individuals and couples out to do mission elsewhere, at the time of writing it's going to be about a year before we send out a church plant. So for wisdom on this, I asked some leaders within the New Wine family who have planted out to share their experience. The following sections include their words, and the wisdom they have gained from being the leader of a donor church.

First, let me briefly introduce them to you:

Linda Maslen planted 'Saturday Gathering' out of a group of people who were coming to faith through a foodbank in Halifax. She went on to multiply to another midweek community, and they planted into another area of Halifax to establish Saturday Gathering West. She moved from Halifax in 2019 to plant Fountains Church in Bradford.

Like Linda, Dave Mitchell has been both a doer and a donor, having been involved in planting around six or seven times. He is senior pastor at Woodlands Church, Bristol, which has planted a number of churches across the city into different contexts.

Ian Parkinson was the leader of All Saints Marple – the church which planted out Glo Central back in 2010. At the time he and Nadine, his wife, were also leading the north and east regions of New Wine, and hosted the New Wine North conferences. He currently works for the Church Pastoral Aid Society (CPAS) as a leadership specialist, equipping those training for ordained ministry.

Finally, Paul Harcourt is the national leader of New Wine England, and he and his wife, Becky, lead All Saints Woodford Wells. They currently oversee a group of seven churches, five of which they planted in the last ten years.

Blessings and Challenges

To lead a church that plants churches brings both blessings and difficulties as you navigate the changes it brings.

There are blessings for the donor church when they choose to step out and plant. These tend to be around the sense of partnering with the Lord in extending the kingdom beyond the local context; opportunities that are created for new people to step up into leadership within the donor church when the planting team has left; and renewing the donor church with a reinvigorated missional mindset.

Paul says that planting has 'challenged us to shift our thinking from consumerism and addition up to discipleship and multiplication. The challenge of multiplying means we're constantly putting a kingdom message before people – we need you: everybody has a gift, everybody needs to play their part.'[2]

Linda agrees. Planting 'created a lot of opportunities for people to grow and develop. It provided that stepping stone for people to go on to do bigger things; it gives people that opportunity to speak, for more people to lead and more people to be involved.'

Ian mentions that 'one of the blessings was simply being obedient', and Dave notes that, 'there's spiritual favour, because God wants us to partner with him, and if you're keeping in step with the Spirit, then God is generous to you'.

Planting helps support a missional imperative in the donor church. According to Dave: 'The mother church has an increased sense of urgency to bring in unchurched people. In doing that, most of us find connecting with people who are not yet Christians highly energising and beneficial to our own faith.'

But there are also challenges for the donor church, just as there are challenges for a mother when giving birth to a child.

Dave describes the feeling of 'postnatal depression' which can occur because the donor church still needs visionaries and givers, but instead that energy often goes into the new church plant. However, he points out, 'It's amazing what God restores.'

The obvious challenge when sending a leader and a team is that the donor church *community* changes significantly.

Linda lost a significant number of the congregation, even though that was always part of the plan.

Both Dave and Paul expect to send around one in ten of the church community for a significant plant. It was a different story for Ian, though, whose church only sent out a handful of people, partly because they were planting into a different cultural context. They therefore needed people who were flexible enough to adapt to a new setting rather than engrained in a particular culture that would be difficult to step beyond.

For the leaders in the donor church, the idea of losing a bunch of great people forces us back to the Father, to find our security not in what we see in front of us, not in what we have built, but in who we are as God's children, following his call and his will. Once again, the ripples are affected by the stone: even this stage demands of us that we allow God to work on the five characteristics in us. We can then become more of the leader he wants us to be, and the kind of leader we want to be: praying, envisioning, growing, acting and learning.

It can affect personal relationships too. Planting churches with others gives 'an intensity to our relationship which will not be sustainable,' says Dave. If they, or you, move on to do something new, it can make some people question if the friendship is genuine if it's so easily lost. Dave has learned to be honest in conversation, communicating to others that a change in the dynamics of a relationship 'doesn't mean to say that how we love you right now isn't real and hasn't got a place in eternity, but it's probably not going to follow through into the next decade in the same way it has been'.

But sending others is not just about losing them, their skills and their leadership from the donor church.

It also has a *financial impact* – people who leave to join the planting team are now investing their time, money and effort into a new church community. This means their giving decreases to the donor church. The donor church may also be investing a financial gift to help the plant in the first couple of years.

In addition to this, there is a *cost around vision* – with all the talk being about the church plant, people within the donor church can wonder if the vision there has stalled. What's the vision for those of us who are staying?

Dave says: 'The sending church also needs to be able to give a vision for what it means to stay and be fruitful, otherwise it's not a level playing field in terms of the calling.'

Paul summarises it this way: 'The costs and challenges have a significant impact in terms of finance, people power and focus – I feel like we've been talking about our two new church plants incessantly over the last few months.'

So the costs are clear, and considerable. But Ian makes the point that 'every decision to start any new ministry implies a decision not to do certain other things. So although there is a cost, it is a decision happily taken – one which was considered to be a positive deployment of resources.'

What strikes you as the most difficult cost in planting? How might you prepare yourself and your church for some of these costs early in the planting journey, so that when you multiply by planting, it's not too much of a shock for everyone? What could you do to help your people own the challenges and celebrate the blessings?

Culture of Generosity

Becoming a donor church is about choosing to be generous, choosing to give away and choosing to embrace the cost of planting for the sake of others.

Growth in the five characteristics will bring an overflow of humility and generosity. You can't multiply if you're looking to keep things just for your own church or vision. Being generous means trusting God will replace what you lose; it means being open-handed and open-hearted; keeping the bigger picture in mind; remembering Jesus said, 'I will build my church' and commanded us to 'seek first the kingdom'.[3]

Building a culture of generosity requires a kingdom mindset. 'We're not empire builders,' explains Dave. 'We're first and foremost a kingdom participant, and church planting is essential if we are going to reach all the communities we are trying to reach. You don't want to kill the goose that lays the golden egg by overplanting, but on the other hand we can't stay still.'

This spirit of generosity means encouraging everyone to consider God's call on their lives: the leaders of the new plant, those who will join them, and those who remain. As Paul says, 'We want people who stay to feel called here, and we want people who go to feel called there.'

Ian suggests that creating a culture of generosity means the church becomes used to giving away resources and people. Linda's church was literally formed out of a community committed to generosity: a foodbank, giving away food to the hungry, and helping them find spiritual nourishment too.

A generous church will also be committed to welcoming newcomers.

Dave does this by always having things for new people: 'We always have welcome, food, connection points, receptions, Alpha, all year round, all the time. It builds a confidence for people: this is a church I could bring my friend to.' Welcoming newcomers and developing a generous culture means people trust that if they are going to invite a friend to a church gathering, they will get a good welcome and others will offer them their time and energy. It also means when an individual happens to stumble into a church gathering, they step into a kind, welcoming community.

Jesus' parable of the sower teaches us to have a generous, open, kingdom expectation: to give away what you have, as an investment that you hope will bear much fruit.

How might you develop a generous culture within your church, so that when the opportunity to plant comes you can respond?

Leadership Pipelines

Being generous means intentionally investing in others to give away what we have ourselves. It means developing a leadership pipeline to raise up and release new leaders.

Nicky Gumbel was once asked how many churches he thought HTB could plant in a year. His answer? It depends how many leaders we have. So, developing a leadership pipeline is vital to any planting or multiplying a church might do. Discipling others, investing in and releasing them, will bring multiplication by raising others up and increasing the impact of what's currently happening, and it will also mean sending others out to start new things.

We've considered in the leading and establishing chapters what it might look like to help someone move from being unconsciously *in*competent to unconsciously competent, and multiplying is the point where those newly developed leaders can stretch their wings and fly.

Referring to how important it is to have good leaders for the church plant, Paul says, 'People go with a leader. Having a leader that is ready, who has had time to cast a vision and draw people around them is key. Those who join the planting team are probably not following a vision for a new church, they've more likely bought into the leader.'

Linda talks about the character required in the leaders of the new plant: 'They need to be really secure in themselves and in their relationship with God, and feel that God is calling them to do something which is new. They need to be prepared to face up to some of the challenges that brings.' The church plant leaders need to embody the five characteristics of praying, envisioning, growing, acting and learning so those attributes can ripple out to others as they plant. The question is, how can you invest in these characteristics in potential church plant leaders?

It's all about discipleship.

A leadership pipeline creates some clear steps for someone to develop their leadership skills, so that they can be as ready as possible to take on leadership themselves. Ian argues that, 'for leaders, it's not about holding too tight on to the people you have but how you can grow them and add value to them'.

'It's essential we create a leadership pipeline that's going to take the church to the next generation,' says Dave. At Woodlands Church, their pipeline starts with an individual taking on small group leadership, then taking some responsibility within Sunday worship, then stepping into being a congregation leader, and then possibly heading out to plant a church.

Leadership development needs to be intentional. 'We can't just assume that those who are planting have a deep understanding of the core DNA,' says Linda. 'When four of our leaders left to plant, I wrote down our DNA and shared it with them so they could see and understand it more clearly.' Having realised that DNA is both caught and taught, she's now also spending more intentional time with people before they plant out.

Dave also believes that part of raising up leaders involves being frank about the cost of planting so planters begin the process with their eyes wide open. Reflecting on his own early experiences of church planting he says, 'We'd just had a new baby, and our four other kids were really small. We'd be out of the house at 8 a.m. on a Sunday; my wife was giving them breakfast as I was setting up PA equipment. We had a low point in our marriage around that year, so it's important to communicate to potential plant leaders: "If you're going to do this thing, it's not a job, it's a lifestyle." As leaders, we need to encourage planters to keep that lifestyle healthy and compatible with what they've been called to do.'

What might a leadership pipeline look like for you? How can you intentionally raise people up into leadership in order that they might be ready to plant out? What steps in increasing responsibility can someone take, and how will you coach and encourage them on the journey towards planting?

Telling the Story

Before planting out, Ian began to raise the general possibility with church members that some might feel called to relocate and be part of the new team even before the plant leaders had been appointed, to get the church ready for the adventure.

Linda recommends frequent and clear communication to the whole church 'about what you're doing, why you're doing it, how you're going to do it and where it's going to be'. This should be done little and often, drip-feeding information along the way. 'It's not like all of a sudden you announce, "We're going to do this big plant, and all of these people are going to leave." Rather, we communicate something along the lines of "we're thinking about, we're praying into ...". Take the church on this journey with you, including the ups and downs, so that everyone feels involved and engaged, even if they decide not to go to the new plant in the end. And of course, you get them praying into it. When they receive prophetic words and pictures, it all helps to shape the direction.'

Although Paul publicly shares with the whole church the vision to plant out, he leaves building the team entirely to the church planters. He looks to the example of Pete and Nicki Sims at Skylark Church, whose church has an amazing history of planting.[4] 'They work on the premise that once the plant has been agreed, the new plant leaders cast the vision and the senior leaders take their hands off the whole thing.'

Dave, however, recommends having one-to-one conversations with some key individuals, particularly those who may have a high level of responsibility in what already exists. Even though they might be excited about joining a planting team, their departure from the donor church is likely to have a huge impact. This isn't to say they shouldn't respond to God's call, but there need to be honest conversations about the possibility of them moving on, and what a healthy process would look like, including a handover period, should they decide to go. It's important the mother church is not damaged long-term by planting out.

Stories help explain not just what, but why. Dave explains that you need to communicate to the church: 'We can't afford *not* to do this.' He goes on to say that testimonies are important to remind people 'of what's already happened because of growth, and also paint the picture of where we're going to and the need that's there'. Ian shared how important testimonies and stories are *after* planting too – encouraging the church about their investment and the fruit that it's bearing for the kingdom of God.

Dave argues that 'if we're not reproducing the small things, the smaller size dynamics or stages, it'll probably be harder to reproduce the whole thing'. For us here at Saint Philips, we use the language of planting, even in relation to our Connect Groups: when a group has grown and needs to multiply, we celebrate and use the language of planting. What we do in the small becomes second nature to us, and when we do it as a whole church, it will feel more normal.

What small thing can you multiply that will give people an appetite for planting? How can you tell the story to help develop a culture of mission and discipleship in your plant, so that when it comes to planting out, people own it for themselves?

Relating to Other Churches

For the leaders of the donor church, communication extends beyond just the people within the church. It's important to get to know the other church leaders in the area in which you are looking to plant. Paul says that the churches in their locality are 'all very different in churchmanship from All Saints' and that 'relational trust and equity' is key. Connecting well with other church leaders helps to develop that trust, as it can feel threatening to have a new church planted nearby. It's important to reassure other local leaders that you are planting for the sake of others, for those who don't yet know Jesus, rather than trying to steal their sheep. But these conversations can only happen in the context of relational trust.

Ian spoke of being particularly careful 'not to do anything that would give other church leaders any ammunition to fire back at us', and working hard to sustain good relationships with those who may feel threatened by the idea of a new church plant.

It is always possible that some other Christians might join the plant from other churches. However, we must always remember that this is not the point of church planting. Dave gathers the church leaders who are part of the New Wine network in Bristol regularly, and he recognises the importance of a kingdom mindset – if one church grows, we all win. 'We acknowledge that transfer growth does happen, but we don't encourage that, and we don't want to destabilise other churches by coming into a region.'

Although you can't control what other people do, you can control the way you go about planting, and seek to honour others who have been working in that particular part of the vineyard already. Aiming for holiness, humility and a focus on the lost may help reduce some of the anxiety and frustration in other church leaders.

If you are working in an established denomination, it can be helpful to invite those to whom you are accountable, the regional leaders, apostolic overseers, bishops, archdeacons etc., to get involved in these conversations too.

Ultimately, however, we don't decide on whether to do something based on whether other people might get upset, but because of the many, many people who don't yet know Jesus, and the prompting of the Holy Spirit to seek first his kingdom.

When to Plant

So you've sought to develop good relationships with other church leaders around you. But how do you, as leader of the donor church, know when it's time to plant?

Ian simply suggests, 'If you wait until you're ready you'll never be ready.' In the 1990s, he had been about to take out a team to plant in a nearby location. The plan was pulled at the last minute because of a nervousness about the impact on the donor church – taking resources away, and a fear that they might not survive. 'It would have survived,' Ian now reflects. 'It was strong numerically and in all kinds of other ways, but the experience made me realise that often churches hold on to resources thinking they need more than they really do.'

Dave talked about being shrewd in determining when to plant, citing Jesus' parables in Luke 14 about a builder counting the cost before starting a new tower, or a king carefully considering the cost of going to war: 'If you're going to build a tower or fight an army, count the cost,' Dave says. 'But, as Jesus said in verse 33, "those of you who do not give up everything you have cannot be my disciples". We've got one life to live; we've got a task to do; it's not finished yet.' It may be costly, and we need to be wise, but we also need to do all we can to share the kingdom of God with others.

It might be that, like Linda, you don't really have a choice about planting because the building is full, and you can't fit anyone else in. Whatever the impetus for planting out, counting the cost means thinking about the finances, the people, the leaders, the geographic or demographic focus, and your ability to help support the plant once they have moved away. It's balancing this with the faith in a generous God who always out-gives us, who brings resurrection out of death, and makes us strong in our weakness.

Where to Plant

We've covered why, what, who, how and when to plant a church. So how do you determine *where* to plant? All five characteristics remain relevant here, but prayer is vital as you discern and work with the Holy Spirit and others to determine where you might best plant out. It's not always straightforward or easy, but it's about discerning the opportunities the Holy Spirit is leading you in, with his strategic direction. Where is he giving you peace about a location to plant? Is he opening the doors or closing them?

As we planted into Chapel Street in Salford, the question of *where* had been decided before we got involved. The bishop's leadership team had identified St Philip's as the largest building they owned near to the city centre and a university, and which was also surrounded by redevelopment plans. Taking into consideration all these factors, it seemed to be an ideal place to start something new.

Similarly, Ian responded to his bishop's prompting, who had realised there was little gospel presence on a social housing estate. It was the bishop who had the vision to plant something new, and it was the archdeacon who worked on the details about how to plant into a different parish, so there was never really a question of *where*.

Dave, who is outside the structures of a denomination, suggests considering the people already in your church. Are there 'people coming from a specific geographical location or representing a particular demographic'? Could this be an indicator of where to plant, so that 'instead of those people coming to you, you go to them'? This is one key way of determining where the Holy Spirit may already be at work.

And that is exactly what Linda did. The leaders of Saturday Gathering did a search based on everyone's postcode. 'This meant we could choose a location that was near to where there was a significant demographic.' A simple review of where people lived was the catalyst for the next stage of finding somewhere for the new church to meet. This was also dependent on the Holy Spirit opening the right door for them. They had an idea of what they were looking for, but he had something else in mind. 'We looked around at every kind of space, but none of them felt like the right places to go.' Finally, they came across a vicar who was excited about the prospect of welcoming them, and they began to meet in his church building.

Paul sensed the nudge of the Spirit when he learned of a vast new housing development in Barking Riverside, and worked with his denomination to consider planting there. Interestingly, this has also impacted the kind of church they are planting, based more around homes than a central gathering space, as there was no church building or community centre in the locality.

It seems determining where to plant is a discernment process that involves both pragmatic and opportunistic decision making – discerning with others what the Holy Spirit is saying.

Ongoing Support

Paul described how the first church they planted out was led by someone who wasn't looking for a huge amount of support; in this instance they commissioned the church plant and wished them well without a continuing relationship. Usually, however, the donor church stays connected to the church they have planted, just as a parent and child will stay close for a season of their life, before the child is adult and ready to take responsibility for their own life. Paul also says he tries to help the doer, the planter, have realistic expectations: 'I think that the stories of rapid growth from day one are the exception rather than the rule.' He suggests ongoing support can help manage these expectations.

Those who have planted out of Paul's church are welcome to join the donor church staff meetings. There are now five or six churches all represented in one staff meeting where they share how they are doing, encourage one another, and then spend time separately on their own plans.

Dave suggests assessing your ability to support and oversee the new church plant – 'Have you got the management and mentoring capacity to see it thrive and flourish?' He continues to meet with a leader who planted four years ago, and laughs, 'I think he's coaching me, really!'

Linda kept supporting the leaders of Saturday Gathering West after they had planted, and often went there herself to help lead and encourage.

Ian's church provided the governance for Glo Church, dealing with the safeguarding, finances, and legal stuff, so the plant was able to concentrate solely on the mission. Ian came to lead communion once a month, but other than this and meeting with the leaders of the plant, he was very open-handed.

What things could you do to support a leader and church plant you've sent out or might one day send out? How might you grow in Christ, in your security in him, as you look to release and send out others? And how might you help your people do the same?

History Makers

The ripples created by a leader and a community that is praying, envisioning, growing, acting and learning can have far-reaching effects. Think about it: the reason you and I are followers of Jesus is because somebody, somewhere, planted a church. In response to prayer, they caught the vision to share their faith with others. They took responsibility to grow in their faith enough to give something a go, and act in the name of Jesus, as they learned about how to share the gospel to a new people group in a new generation. And a little church was born.

There are records of a church on the site of St Mary's, Stockport from 1190, and the stone chancel from 1360 still remains. St Mary's was the grandmother church of Glo Church; in 1588, St Mary's planted All Saints church in Marple, which was a village at the time, about five miles away. In 2010, All Saints planted Glo into Offerton. It took nearly a thousand years for the mission in Stockport to ripple out to the Offerton estate through Glo Church.[5]

In Manchester, there is evidence of a church building from the seventh century, and it's possible in AD 923 there was a building where the cathedral now stands.[6] In 1822, when the church commissioners invested a huge amount of money into building churches in response to rapid urbanisation, the cathedral planted St Philip's, Salford.

In 2016, when we planted Saint Philips Chapel Street, there were around 2.1 million people living in the Manchester diocese. With a generous estimate that around 5 per cent of people worship in a church on a Sunday, that still leaves 2 million people without a relationship with Jesus expressed through the local church.

With so many people without a living faith in Jesus, I believe church planting is a key component of seeking God's kingdom in the here and now: the Holy Spirit working in us and through us, leading, relating, incarnating, establishing and multiplying the life of faith he brings.

It's our turn now. We can be grateful to those who planted churches in the past and spend our time tweaking church to be just the way we like it. Or, inspired by our forebears, we can play our part in reaching those who don't know Jesus and sharing his invitation with them.

It's not easy. There'll be bumps along the way, but I want to invite you:

To take up your cross and follow Jesus.

To find your treasure in heaven, not here on earth.

To invest yourself in the eternal, not the temporary.

To use this book as a rough guide to help make a big kingdom impact as you throw yourself into the unknown, say yes to the Holy Spirit, and cause kingdom ripples to flow out, impacting generations to come.

Giving Birth

I was around when Lizzy gave birth to all three of our gorgeous children. From what I remember, it hurt her quite a lot. (For our third child, Lizzy decided not to use any pain relief, and did Pilates exercises every day to get ready for it. The doctors and nurses in the baby unit came to give her a round of applause afterwards!)

There's a lot of screaming. There are facial expressions you never thought possible. Any sense of dignity is thrown out the window – as a whole bunch of people in the room are staring at a part of your body that is normally extremely private. And it goes on.

For hours.

Pain. Sweat. Difficulty. Wanting to give up.

And then the baby cries, and everything changes.

Three times I've seen this happen: agony changed to elation. Suffering turned to joy.

Multiplying is painful. It's costly. It can take a lot of time and energy to invest in someone or something new.

But it's always worth it.

It's the way of *life*.

Afterword

Alan Hirsch

Stones and ripples ... this image of an originating action that has ongoing effects lends itself very well to the idea of *movement*. And I don't mind admitting I have been known to be somewhat obsessed with movements! I believe the recovery of movement-making and movement-thinking is absolutely critical to the advance of Christianity in the twenty-first century and beyond. So, permit me to add some more movemental wisdom to this already wise book.

First, remember, it is Jesus who is the ultimate Stone, and we (the church) are some of the ripples. The metaphor reminds us that the original and originating impact that started things off in the first place is a particular person with a particular calling and a particular way: King Jesus. It is Jesus who is our Founder and our Leader; Jesus is the Author and Perfecter of our faith. To be true to our identity and calling, we must never, not even for a moment, forget that this is the movement that Jesus started, and it exists to extend his mission and purposes in the world. Therefore, every authentic expression of the church – be it a church plant or a denominational organisation or anything in between – must be based squarely on Jesus' saving work on our behalf. It needs to remain committed to his explicit commands and teachings, and it must act in conformity with him from the very beginning to the very end. The church needs to act, look, sound and think like Jesus if it is to be an authentic church. Let's call this *the Jesus effect*, and it is the most critical factor in any form of Christian mission.

Second, and somewhat ironically, can I suggest you don't actually plant churches. We are never told to plant churches in the Scriptures. Rather, you should *plant the gospel, the Jesus story*, among a certain people group, and it is Jesus who will build his church to suit.[1] If we fail to recognise the priority of the gospel itself, then we will likely start with a prefabricated understanding of the church, and we will fail to create genuinely contextualised (incarnational) expressions of the church. The way I explain this in my book *The Forgotten Ways* is to say that it is Christology (the phenomenon of Jesus the Founder) that informs our missiology (our sense of purpose and our methodology) that in turn shapes our ecclesiology (the forms and expressions of the church). If we fail to heed this pattern, then the churches we plant will all tend to end up looking like the same, tired, worn-out European forms with clergy, steeples and pews. Do the prior work of incarnational mission and evangelism, and the church will emerge out of that.

And third, can I suggest (again) you don't plant churches. Rather, you should plant movements instead. It is important we begin with the end in mind. If we want to be part of the 'pay-it-forward' movement – the church that Jesus intended us to be – then we need to start with a movemental idea of church in the first place. If we don't do this, then we will not start a church that can, or will even desire to, multiply. Movements are adaptive and can go on to scale and multiply, and they activate all authentic disciples in the task of Jesus' mission, not just a professional clergy. Start with the end in mind, and you will find yourself in the movement that Jesus started, the movement that is always changing the world.

And finally, consider these words of movemental wisdom by Roland Allen, one of the greatest Anglican missionaries of all time:

> The spontaneous expansion of the Church reduced to its elements is a very simple thing. It asks for no elaborate organization, no large finances, no great numbers of paid missionaries. In its beginning it may be the work of one man, and that of a man neither learned in the things of this world, nor rich in the wealth of this world ... What is necessary is faith. What is needed is the kind of faith which, uniting a man to Christ, sets him on fire.[2]

Acknowledgements

This book would not have been possible without the help of many people. (I always used to read that in other people's books, and think, how many people does it take to help bring a book together?! Well, now I know.)

The pioneers and planters who shared their principles on our Pioneer and Planter Days in Manchester: this book literally would not exist without you. Same goes for Jenny Richardson who helped collate and work on these principles; and Philip James and David Jennings making the investment in this research and giving huge support to us from the Church Commissioners.

The people who have been on our various teams and journeyed with us as we've learned through our successes and mistakes: thank you for putting up with us, loving us and serving alongside us. These stories are your stories. And of course, huge thanks to the donor church leaders without whom there would only be a very short chapter on multiplying.

The amazing group of people that is New Wine: in particular Paul and Becky Harcourt and the leadership team, for cheering us on in planting, and in writing this book. Thanks to Dave Hase who has worked hard with 100 Movements on things that make no sense to me.

The people who have cheered me on while I was writing: Jo Saxton who read first initial ideas and encouraged me to flesh them out; Winfield Bevins for recognising I needed to get this written down before taking on anything new; those who read the first draft; those who gave helpful feedback; my church community here at Saint Philips Chapel Street; and various bishops along the way, notably Ric Thorpe, Mark Ashcroft and Jill Duff. Thanks also to the Manchester Diocesan team under Bishop David Walker as we planted a resource church here in the city centre. Bob and Mary Hopkins need a mention as they've been relentlessly encouraging us in our planting and as we try to help others.

The team at 100 Movements Publishing: I'm so grateful to Anna Robinson (no relation, except in Christ) who's had the unenviable task of being my editor. This book is so much better because of your help and input. Thanks to Kate Lehane for the cover idea, and to those I haven't met but who have helped pull the rest of the design and edit together.

And finally, my amazing family: Lizzy, my wife, my partner, my love. Thanks for doing this adventure called life with me. To the kids: Daisy, Lucy and Toby, thanks for coming along for the ride. I know you didn't always have a choice, but you have always chosen to throw yourselves into what the Lord was inviting us to do, and have grown through it. I couldn't be prouder of you. Go on to do even greater things in Jesus' name.

Notes

Introduction: How We Got Here

1 A missional community is a group of Christians who have a shared vision
   to demonstrate and proclaim the good news of Jesus to a particular place
   or people group. They look to connect with, and create space for, those
   outside of the church wanting to explore faith. It is usually part of a larger
   church congregation.
2 A learning community is a gathering of people in a particular field, in this
   instance church leaders, pioneers and planters, to share ideas and learn
   together, with a particular focus. Learning communities are used across
   many professions and are one of the ways church networks can collaborate
   and learn together.
3 Jim Collins, *Good to Great* (first ed.) (New York: Random House Business,
   2001).
4 A resource church is a church within the Church of England that has a
   specific remit to plant other churches. It is given additional resources to a
   normal parish church, in order that it may then be a resource by planting
   out other churches.

Section One (Preliminaries)

1 Hebrews 12:2.
2 John 1:1–2.
3 Mark 3:21.
4 Isaiah 6:3.
5 Luke 9:58.
6 Philippians 2:6–11.
7 Hebrews 12:2.
8 Hebrews 12:3.
9 James 5:16.
10 Leviticus 16.

11 Deuteronomy 32:51.
12 Leviticus 11:44, 45; 19:2; 20:26.
13 1 Peter 1:14–16.
14 1 Peter 2:11.
15 Philippians 3:20.
16 Hebrews 4:15.
17 Luke 10:27.
18 Matthew 28:19–20.
19 1 Peter 2:9.

1 Praying

1   Spoken at a seminar at New Wine.
2   Luke 11:1.
3   Luke 5:16.
4   Read the full story in 1 Samuel 1:1–18.
5   1 Samuel 1:10.
6   Ephesians 6:18.
7   Philippians 4:6.
8   Matthew 6:9–13.
9   Matthew 7:8.
10 Luke 11:13.
11 Luke 18:7.
12 See Isaiah 53:12 and 1 Timothy 2:1.
13 See https://www.merriam-webster.com/dictionary/interceding#other-words.
14 Romans 8:34.
15 Romans 8:26.
16 Acts 16:7.
17 Colossians 3:15.
18 Ibid.
19 Acts 16:9. Macedonia is northern Greece.
20 Dr Rowan Williams, 'Archbishop's Presidential Address – General
    Synod, York, July 2003', *Dr Rowan Williams 104th Archbishop of Canterbury*,
    14 July 2003, http://aoc2013.brix.fatbeehive.com/articles.php/1826/
    archbishops-presidential-address-general-synod-york-july-2003.
21 John 5:19.
22 Quoted in John Stott, *Between Two Worlds: The Challenge of Preaching Today* (Grand
    Rapids: Eerdmans, 1994), 111.

23 Colossians 3:15–16.
24 Housefires, 'Good Good Father', by Tony Brown and Pat Barrett, 2015.
    Produced by Ed Cash, Jeremy Edwardson and Ross Copperman.
25 1 Kings 19:12.
26 Compline is one of the historic daily offices which is prayed before bedtime,
    allowing reflection on the day, some words of confession, and asking God
    for safety through the night.

2 Envisioning

1 I adore Charles Wesley's brief but stunning way of summing up
   chapters 9–11 in Romans and demonstrating Jesus as the fulfilment of
   all God's promises in the Old Testament in his hymn 'Come, Thou Long
   Expected Jesus', when he writes, 'Israel's strength and consolation'.
   Genius.
2 David Bosch, *Transforming Mission: Paradigm Shifts in Theology of Mission*
   (Maryknoll: Orbis, 1991).
3 Read the story in Nehemiah 1–7.
4 Well, apart from his life being at risk every time he went to work … He was
   cupbearer to the king so had to taste any drink before the king drank it, in
   case it was poisoned …
5 See Nehemiah 4:14.
6 See Nehemiah 4:4–5; 6:9, 6:14.

3 Growing

1 Miley Cyrus, 'The Climb', by Jessi Alexander and Jon Mabe, 2009.
   Produced by Jon Shanks, Hollywood Records Inc.
2 It's been said that what happened physically in the Old Testament is often
   a good picture of what happens spiritually in Christ. We can take from
   this that the Lord wants to use people to help bring freedom to others by
   fighting against oppression.
3 Judges 5:15–17.
4 A little pop reference from my youth. Hello, 1980s' pop fans.
5 Judges 4:6–7.
6 Judges 4:8.
7 Paraphrase of Psalm 137:9.

8   Romans 8:28 was a regular promise we were praying through at the time.

9   Mark 1:15.

10   Peter Scazzero's book, *The Emotionally Healthy Leader: How transforming your inner life will deeply transform your church, team, and the world* (Grand Rapids: Zondervan, 2015), has been incredibly helpful in the area of emotional health. If you haven't already, I highly recommend reading it.

11   David Benner, ed., *Baker Encyclopedia of Psychology* (Grand Rapids: Baker, 1985), quoted in Valerie J. McIntyre, *Sheep in Wolves' Clothing: How unseen need destroys friendship and community and what to do about it* (Grand Rapids: Baker, 1999), 34.

12   McIntyre, *Sheep in Wolves' Clothing*, 38.

13   Stephen R. Covey, *The 7 Habits of Highly Effective People: Restoring the Character Ethic* (New York: Simon & Schuster, 1992).

14   Check out John Mark Comer's *The Ruthless Elimination of Hurry: How to stay emotionally healthy and spiritually alive in the chaos of the modern world* (London: Hodder & Stoughton, 2019) if you haven't already. It's a challenging but important book.

4 Acting

1   The story starts in Genesis 37.

2   Genesis 39:3–4.

3   Genesis 39.

4   Genesis 39:20–23.

5   This was completely unexpected, and we were amazed to win. They highlight some fantastic projects going on around our country, https://www.cinnamonnetwork.co.uk.

6   Just for the record, I'm not. But I'm trying to get better.

7   NBA.com Staff, 'Legends profile: Michael Jordan', https://www.nba.com/history/legends/profiles/michael-jordan.

8   Luke 10:2.

9   Luke 10:3.

10   Luke 9:23.

11   Luke 10:10–11.

12   The Greek word 'Satan' means 'accuser'.

13   2 Corinthians 10:5.

5 Learning

1   And they plant churches too, with a guide that could be written for church planters. Since 2013 they have planted into forty-four other locations around the world. See https://www.sundayassembly.com.
2   John 16:13. Note the word 'you' here is plural in the Greek: he will guide you, together, into all the truth.
3   1 Corinthians 12:7.
4   Ephesians 4:11–13.
5   Luke 4:32.
6   Luke 5:5.
7   Luke 6:13.
8   Proverb popularised by Stan Lee's *Spider-Man* comic books. See Wikipedia, 'With great power comes great responsibility', https://en.wikipedia.org/wiki/With_great_power_comes_great_responsibility.
9   Luke 9:2.
10   Luke 9:13.
11   Luke 9:21.
12   John 15:15.
13   Luke 12:32.
14   Matthew 16:23.
15   Acts 1:8.
16   Matthew 28:20.
17   Acts 5:38–39.
18   Neil Cole, *Organic Leadership: Leading Naturally Right Where You Are* (Grand Rapids: Baker Books, 2010), 254.
19   For example, see 'Why Google rewards its employees for failing', *Blueprint Creative*, 8 January 2018, https://blueprintcreativeinc.com/why-google-rewards-its-employees-for-failing.
20   See https://www.5lovelanguages.com/quizzes/.
21   Gary Chapman, *The 5 Love Languages: The Secret to Love That Lasts* (Chicago: Moody Press, 2009).

Section Two (Preliminaries)

1   John 15:16.
2   1 Timothy 3:1–7.
3   Mark 10:45.

4   Miroslav Volf and Matthew Croasmun, *For the Life of the World: Theology that Makes a Difference* (Grand Rapids: Brazos Press, 2019), 61.

6 Leading

1   Jeff Haden, 'Top 50 Leadership and Management Experts', *Inc.*, https://www.inc.com/jeff-haden/the-top-50-leadership-and-management-experts-mon.html.

2   John C. Maxwell, *The 21 Irrefutable Laws of Leadership: Follow Them and People Will Follow You* (Nashville: Thomas Nelson, 1998), 11.

3   Steven Skiena and Charles B. Ward, 'Who's Biggest? The 100 Most Significant Figures in History', *Time*, 10 December 2013, https://ideas.time.com/whos-biggest-the-100-most-significant-figures-in-history.

4   Gene Hammett, 'Jack Welch Always Wanted His Team Members to Take Ownership of Their Work. Here's Why', *Inc.*, www.inc.com/gene-hammett/3-lessons-from-jack-welch-on-leadership-that-you-dont-learn-in-business-school.html.

5   Acts 15:36–41.

6   Romans 12:18.

7   Romans 8:28. Interestingly, despite Paul and Barnabas falling out about him, 'John Mark' is likely the same 'Mark' that Paul later mentions in 2 Timothy 4:11 as being 'helpful to me in my ministry'. So perhaps it wasn't a permanent parting of ways in the end!

8   2 Timothy 1:15.

9   Acts 16:1; 2 Timothy 1:5.

10   It doesn't appear to be Paul's normal practice, see Galatians 2:3 – he never insisted Titus needed to be circumcised.

11   1 Timothy 4:7–8.

12   Edwin H. Friedman, *A Failure of Nerve: Leadership in the Age of the Quick Fix*, (New York: Church Publishing Inc., Kindle edition).

13   Friedman describes a 'new orientation toward relational processes as the basis for what I call "leadership through self-differentiation" [which] focuses leaders on themselves rather than on their followers, and on the nature of their presence'. Friedman, *A Failure of Nerve*, kindle location 525.

14   John 13:14–17.

15   Eugene H. Peterson, *Under the Unpredictable Plant: An Exploration in Vocational Holiness* (Grand Rapids: William B Eerdmans, 1996).

16   Morning prayer is one of the three daily offices used historically and globally

in many church traditions including the Church of England. It includes readings from the Psalms, Old Testament and New Testament, and some prayers.

17 Peterson, *Under the Unpredictable Plant*.

18 And we've found out that, because of this, our 'no low' song is now sung all around the world in different families!

19 John 6:66 (I've sometimes wondered if the numbering of this verse was intentional ...).

20 Revelation 12:11.

21 1 Timothy 4:12.

22 Matthew 4:19.

23 Luke 5:1–11.

24 Luke 12:32.

25 Matthew 14:15–21.

26 1 Corinthians 4:16.

27 1 Corinthians 4:17.

28 Matthew 28:16–20.

29 John 14:26.

7 Relating

1 Acts 13:1–3.

2 Acts 13:5.

3 This is all from a fabulous TED talk by Derek Sivers which is now a YouTube video – it's only three-minutes long and *definitely* worth watching. Derek Sivers, 'First Follower: Leadership Lessons from Dancing Guy', 11 February 2010, https://youtu.be/fW8amMCVAJQ.

4 Ibid.

5 I've used the tests on www.fivefoldministry.com to help introduce people to these concepts.

6 A quick search can find you plenty of these tests online for free, though in my experience they become more useful to everyone when you have an expert help the whole team understand more about themselves and each other. It's a worthwhile investment of resources.

7 It's devastatingly sad about the credible accusations made against Hybels while leading Willow Creek Community Church. I'm not of the opinion, however, that if he is guilty we should ignore everything he said. He taught some good principles, even if he wasn't able to live up to the standards he suggested for others. And I pray for grace for me and you, to be able to

walk the narrow path, so that what we lead doesn't become discredited by our own brokenness. He wrote about the '3 Cs' in *Courageous Leadership* (Grand Rapids: Zondervan, 2002), 80–85.

8   See Judges 7.

9   The difference between them and the Spartans popularised in the amazing 2007 film *300* directed by Zack Snyder was that these three hundred had the Lord on their side and won a mighty victory.

10   Matthew 18:15–17.

11   Matthew 7:3.

12   Matthew 7:1–2.

13   John 13:34.

14   For more on this, check out Carol Tavris and Elliot Aronson, *Mistakes Were Made (But Not by Me): Why We Justify Foolish Beliefs, Bad Decisions and Hurtful Acts* (London: Pinter & Martin, 2020).

15   Matthew 7:1–5.

16   1 Peter 4:8.

8 Incarnating

1   Visit https://freshexpressions.org.uk for dozens of stories of contextualised mission at work.

2   In the Anglican Church, this is expressed in the words spoken at ordination, reminding us that 'the Church is called upon to proclaim afresh in each generation' our faith in Jesus Christ. See https:// www.churchofengland. org/prayer-and-worship/worship-texts-and-resources/common-worship/ ministry/declaration-assent.

3   For more on this, read the excellent *Disappearing Church* by Mark Sayers.

4   Of course this means they're also likely to consider other church 'brands' too.

5   Though what's engaging for me might look different to what's engaging for someone else – hence lots of different church principles and practices, and worship styles.

6   See Martin Saunders, 'If necessary use words … What did Francis of Assisi really say?' *Christianity Today*, 28 August 2017, https://christiantoday.com/ article/if-necessary-use-words-what-did-francis-of-assisi-really-say/112365. htm

7   2 Timothy 4:5.

8   Romans 10:14.

9   Ephesians 4:11–12.
10 2 Timothy 4:5.
11 John 6:66.
12 See www.message.org.uk/category/eden/.
13 Acts 17:22–31.
14 Acts 17:21.
15 Again, I'd argue that *Disappearing Church* is a must-read for those of us in post-Christian contexts.

9 Establishing

1   Bosch, *Transforming Mission*, 168.
2   Acts 18:19.
3   Acts 19:1–7.
4   Acts 19:9.
5   Acts 20:2.
6   Acts 20:28.
7   Nathan Brewer, *The Pulse of Christ: A Fivefold Training Manual* (Revised and Expanded) (Cody: 100 Movements Publishing, 2020), 43. The concept of 'Start and Go' and 'Stay and Grow' teams was drawn from Neil Cole with Paul Kaak, Phil Helfer, Dezi Baker and Ed Waken, *Primal Fire: Reigniting the Church with the Five Gifts of Jesus* (Carol Stream: Tyndale Momentum, 2014).
8   Gary Thomas, *When to Walk Away: Finding Freedom from Toxic People* (Grand Rapids: Zondervan, 2019), 75.
9   Joseph Myers, *The Search to Belong: Rethinking Intimacy, Community and Small Groups* (Grand Rapids: Zondervan, 2003).
10 James 5:16.
11 Christian A. Schwarz, *Natural Church Development: A Guide to Eight Essential Qualities of Healthy Churches* (US ed.) (St Charles: ChurchSmart Resources, 1996), 32.
12 Luke 9:1–6.
13 Luke 10:1.
14 Joseph, called Justus, and Matthias – the two people suggested to replace Judas Iscariot in the Twelve – were likely part of this group (Acts 1:23).
15 An interesting book on this is Gordon MacKenzie, *Orbiting the Giant Hairball: A Corporate Fool's Guide to Surviving with Grace* (New York: Viking, 1998).
16 Acts 15:1–21.

10 Multiplying

1   Matthew 13:1–23; Mark 4:1–20; Luke 8:4–15.
2   Here, *consumerism* in church means people coming along for what they can get, rather than what they can give. *Addition* means slow growth by just a few people doing the work of multiplying and seeing people join in ones or twos. *Discipleship* in church means everyone playing their part, using their gifts. *Multiplication* is all those disciples doing what this whole chapter is about!
3   Matthew 16:18 and Matthew 6:33.
4   See https://skylarkchurch.com.
5   St Alban's, Offerton was planted in 1893, and has ministered faithfully there ever since. The point stands, though: even with St Alban's, it still took around eight hundred years for the church to ripple out from Stockport to Offerton.
6   See https://www.manchestercathedral.org/learn/about-us/timeline/.

Afterword

1   Matthew 16:18.
2   Roland Allen, *The Spontaneous Expansion of the Church* (Oregon: Wipf and Stock Publishers, 1997), 29–30.

66

We want to see God's Kingdom
break through on earth and,
ultimately, the nations changed 99

**New Wine is a movement of local churches with a shared vision
to see renewal through the ministry of the Holy Spirit.**

Through training, mentoring and planting – delivered through local
churches and church leaders – we want to see God's Kingdom
break through on earth and, ultimately, the nations changed.

Reframation

Seeing God, People, and Mission Through Reenchanted Frames

Alan Hirsch & Mark Nelson

Reframation is a passionate manifesto, calling followers of Jesus to reframe and reenchant our worldview, enlarging our perception of God and gospel. It's an invitation to stretch our minds, expand our hearts, and awaken ourselves and those around us to the grand story of God.

Rooted in Scripture and drawing on poetry, literature, the arts, philosophy, and pop culture, *Reframation* refuses to settle for pious platitudes, and appeals to each and every one of us to experience and articulate the good news narrative in ways that resonate with the spiritual hunger and longings of those in our contemporary culture.

"A timely book for the current flattened, frightened world in which we live."
—**WALTER BRUEGGEMANN**

"Whimsically beautiful and stunningly thoughtful."—**LINDA BERGQUIST**

"Packed with eye-opening and potentially life-transforming insights."—**GREGORY A. BOYD**

"In a time when more people are turning away from the church, *Reframation* helps us rediscover the beauty of the gospel and artfully extend it to those who need it the most."—**GABE LYONS**

Life Out Loud

Joining Jesus Outside the Walls of the Church

Rowland Smith

As pastor and worship leader Rowland Smith started to join Jesus outside the walls of the church—in everyday places with everyday people—he discovered an exciting and dynamic faith.

Soundly framed by practical theology, personal reflection, and experiential knowledge, Rowland charts a course we can all walk, and invites you to discover an adventurous life with Jesus—your own life out loud.

"Read this if you want to better understand what it looks like to engage God's redemptive mission in the places you live, work, and play."—**BRAD BRISCO**

"Full of practical wisdom and missional insights." —**ALAN AND DEBRA HIRSCH**

"An invitation that reminded me of Jesus on every page."—**BRIAN SANDERS**

"A refreshing read that lightens the religious load."—**HUGH HALTER**

---

info@100Mpublishing.com I www.100Mpublishing.com

Ready or Not
Kingdom Innovation for a Brave New World
Doug Paul

There was a time when Christians pioneered the future—from business to church, mathematics to justice reform. Along the way, that redemptive, adaptive movement became change averse and frozen in time. But ready or not, the invitation is for kingdom leaders to reclaim their calling to innovate.

Weaving together stories with surprising twists, studies with striking conclusions, and spellbinding cultural analysis, Doug Paul unlocks the five phases of kingdom innovation and reveals that whenever God's people have leaned into innovation, the world has shifted on its axis.

"Prepare to be surprised and delighted, and ultimately, roused to action." —**MARK BATTERSON**

"Provocative and compelling, this is an essential book to help us meet the moment." —**WILL MANCINI**

"*Ready or Not* teaches us how to rediscover Christianity's core DNA of innovative creativity—and at just the right time." —**TOD BOLSINGER**

Uptick
A Blueprint for Finding and Forming the Next Generation of Pioneering Kingdom Leaders
John Chandler

In our rapidly changing world, churches need to shape people for adaptive leadership, and we especially need this formation to impact young leaders, who may go on to influence both church and society for decades to come.

Packed with insights and ideas, *Uptick* will enable you to become more effective in developing missionally minded, kingdom leaders, whatever your context.

"Essential reading for anyone seeking to invest in a fresh generation of leaders, and a valuable resource." —**JO SAXTON**

"If you want to help the church live the future in the present, pick up this book."—**JR WOODWARD**

"Any one looking to develop mature, kingdom-focused disciples needs to read this guide." —**DR. AMY L. SHERMAN**

"*Uptick* is a veritable treasure trove, a manifesto of movemental wisdom and ought to become a classic, definitive text." —**ALAN AND DEBRA HIRSCH**

---

info@100Mpublishing.com I www.100Mpublishing.com